PLAIN CLOTHES & SLEUTHS

A HISTORY OF DETECTIVES IN BRITAIN

PLAIN CLOTHES & SLEUTHS

A HISTORY OF DETECTIVES IN BRITAIN

STEPHEN WADE

TEMPUS

First published 2007

Tempus Publishing Limited
The Mill, Brimscombe Port,
Stroud, Gloucestershire, GL5 2QG
www.tempus-publishing.com

British Library Cataloguing in Publication Data.
A catalogue record for this book is available from the British Library.

ISBN 978 0 7524 4186 3

Typesetting and origination by Tempus Publishing Limited
Printed in Great Britain

CONTENTS

INTRODUCTION

In August 2006, a story in *The Times* revealed that a cold case murder of 1967 had been solved: two men were being held and had been charged with the killing of Keith Lyon, a boy who was stabbed eleven times in the chest and back as he walked on the Sussex Downs. Why had this taken so long to solve, and for closure to come, sadly after the deaths of the boy's parents? As *The Times* explained: 'The lost evidence was discovered in 2002 when a group of workmen upgrading a sprinkler system' found a box containing vital evidence. This box had been misplaced in 1967.

This is exactly the type of story that has always created a doggedly persistent ambiguity in the public's view of the police detective: on the one hand a Holmes-like genius of observation and deduction and on the other a bungler who makes basic mistakes that cost lives and reputations. It was always the same, since the creation of the detective force in 1842, and even before then when the Bow Street Runners and Patrol tried their hands at detective work.

The police detective has also had to suffer the eclipse of his actual work and nature by the literary detective, a creation of mythic status. In 1960, Christopher Pilling wrote that Chesterton's Father Brown had a point when he said that 'Ours is the only trade in which the professional is always supposed to be wrong.' Pilling added, 'Intuition may be a long way off legal proof: sometimes now we are taken right through the trial, instead of finishing with the arrest in detective fiction, when the detective can say he has lost interest and go back to his violin … '

This book seeks to counteract these social mediations, recounting the creation of the first detective force in Sir Robert Peel's new police, and taking in some account of how the actual professionals measured against Dickens's inventions and of course, Conan Doyle's Sherlock Holmes. It was a long and arduous struggle to shape a detective branch: in their first phase they were highly suspicious, as any whiff of plain clothes activity suggested the kind of nasty business undertaken by *agents provocateurs* in the dark days of Chartism and working class radicalism. Men in plain clothes had infiltrated the ranks of desperate mill-workers who had bought firearms in the suburbs of the industrial cities of the north, and they met in pubs and inns to hatch their plots of subversion. Among them had been officers of the government, drinking and joking, while all the time noting names and places, dates and intentions.

Peel, in his Police Act of 1829, was not starting from a complete void – there had been professional administrators who had made some moves towards a streamlined metropolitan police well before Peel's time as Home Secretary. In the middle years of the eighteenth century, the novelist Henry Fielding and his blind brother John, along with other various military men, had made some notable steps forward in this context. But the change from a small force patrolling London at night and night watchmen in their booths, to armed and disciplined officers organised in a military fashion, was an immense leap forward. One handbill of 1830 raises most of the issues emerging at the time through fear and distortion:

> Ask yourselves the following question: Why is an Englishman, if he complains of an outrage or an insult, referred for redress to a Commissioner of Police? Why are the proceedings of this new POLICE COURT unpublished and unknown? And by what law of the land is it recognised?

The aims of this social history are manifold. I want to look again at the men involved in this steady evolution of detective science and to ask questions about how they learned their trade and how the systems needed to protect them eventually evolved. Police work on a beat system is perilous in the extreme, and many police murders in the first decade of the new force show this vulnerability. My discussion of the P.C. Clark case (1846) in Chapter 4 highlights this world of danger they lived in day-to-day. But the real fascination is what Dickens understood, as he expressed in his piece, 'A Detective Police Party', from *Household Words* in 1850:

> From these topics, we glide into a review of the most celebrated and horrible of the great crimes that have been committed within the last fifteen or twenty years. The men engaged in the discovery of almost all of them, and in pursuit or apprehension of the murderers, are here, down to the very last instance.

In other words, Dickens saw the magnetic fascination of the public with such men. The sensational murders of the first decades of the detective force – both in London and in the provinces – were major media narratives, and yet the men who pursued the villains were not well known. The detective does not want to be a celebrated person. He wants to enjoy the advantages of being anonymous, of course. But many of the men Dickens met and wrote about were also former military men and so very much accustomed to doing their duty and not crowing about it.

In an age when the penny dreadful magazines and street publications made murder narratives immensely popular (and lucrative for the publishers and vendors) the new interest of a professional force of men in pursuit was a high profile element in the genre. Formerly, the stories, as in the very popular *Newgate Calendar* for instance, focused on the villains and their adventures, from crime to scaffold in many cases. These stories, first issued in 1773, were republished in the 1820s. They told the rip-roaring adventures of such highwaymen and robbers as Dick Turpin and Jack Shepherd. Now, writers and publishers had a whole new dimension of crime narrative to exploit. The detective was at the core of this new media production.

Much of the following account of the birth and growth of the detective in England is necessarily concerned with a process of learning, and this has different planes of interest. First there is the everyday strategy for coping with crime on a grand scale. This meant a gradual development of arms, teamwork and logistics. Then there is the ongoing struggle for the individual of talent working within a system, an organisation. At first the organisation was like a regiment – men were sacked regularly for the same misdemeanours for which they would have been flogged or court-martialled in the armed forces. Later, individuals could specialise, as forensic science progressed. Certain advances were stunningly revolutionary for the profession, notably fingerprinting at the end of the nineteenth century and of course, in my circumscribed period, the special elements such as the Flying Squad and the Fraud Squad.

Ironically, when the police force was being formed in England, the founding father of crime detection, Eugene Vidocq, was in England. He did visit the prisons of Pentonville, Newgate and Millbank, but he was really in London to organise an exhibition. He wanted to be a showman, not a professional adviser. As James Morton has commented in his biography of Vidocq: 'Not only was he on the premises during opening hours but he also put on a little production in which he appeared in various disguises, to the delight of the audience ... ' He had arrived in London three years after the detective force was formed, and had played no part in the detective policies; he had, however, been in London in 1835 to advise on prison discipline. He was a man who had known the worst prisons in France, as a prisoner as well as in his role as police officer. In 1845 he was thinking of starting up a detective agency, extending the one he had in France, but this was clearly not his real motive for being there.

Finally, there is the question of the whole range of other contexts in which the detective has moved, as his need for greater knowledge has increased. However fantastic and far-fetched we find Sherlock Holmes to be, Conan Doyle did understand the need to have knowledge of esoteric areas of life inherent in detective work. The basic skills of filing, classifying, noting observations and memorising faces and biographies is there in Holmes. The first detectives appear to have kept an immense amount of local information in their heads as they walked the streets, cultivating contacts and 'grasses'.

This process of absorbing a body of knowledge involved amateur science in all kinds of affairs. A detective in the Victorian period had to constantly add to his geographical and trade knowledge. He also had to be familiar with a complex street slang and code of behaviour.

In the twentieth century, after the revision of the detective training curriculum in the 1930s, we have the emergence of the 'star' sleuths. These were the men the newspapers loved. Popular film and fiction had made figures such as Fabian of the Yard and Sexton Blake the epitome of the flash, showy, intelligent gentleman, an officer type who was part Holmes but part slick modern man, an habitué of parties, hotels and high-level meetings with 'top brass'. Of course, there was capital punishment until 1964, and so these new detectives with impressive credentials and equally notable cars were called on to travel into the regions and help the local bobbies. This gave the newspapers yet more fodder for their sensationalism and love of personal trivia when they made a professional into a media star.

The overall course of the evolution of the detective in England has been one of steady acquisition of a range of professional skills, but at the heart of this dangerous, challenging and unhealthy profession is an armoury of abilities that defy definition, ranging from instinct to incisive logic. The 'nose' of the true sleuth was learned by bumbling – naïve trial and error. The streets and their turbulent, complex network of crime and criminals taught the detective how the business of crime works. In one of the early cases of the murder of a policeman – the second murdered officer after the 1829 Act – P.C. Long was knifed in Charing Cross Road and a man arrested and eventually hanged on the slenderest of details, mainly that he wore a brown coat and a witness had said the killer wore a brown coat. Place that by the side of the incredibly complex investigations of a late twentieth-century murder case, when the trappings of science and professional procedure dominate every step of the police work, and the historical process is perceived clearly.

When Leonard 'Nipper' Read, the man who caught the Krays, was finally induced to write his memoirs (with the help of James Morton) he paid tribute to the man who had taught him the detective's trade, Martin Walsh. What Read had to say about Walsh is arguably the clearest definition of standard and successful detective work ever expressed. Read said:

He was, without doubt, the most dedicated man I have ever met. Everyone knew his qualities. He was tenacious and persistent. The words could almost have been coined to describe him. He would sit, and have me sit with him, for hours on end observing a suspect. He would watch someone leave a building and say 'he'll be back.' When after a few hours I would say, as an impatient 22-year-old, that we had blown it, he would reply, 'Give it a bit longer.' ... Sure enough, the man would return.

The detective needs some kind of challenge and competition to keep improving and to put up with the waiting and the boredom of the job. Martin Walsh had made that tedious element of the work his motivation and his professionalism. In the first two decades of the new detective police, the most likely reason why skills were sharpened and expertise developed was the fact that the Bow Street Patrol that the detectives in Bow Street commanded were still there, some alongside the new officers, as rivals.

One of the main barriers to progress at first was the social and political context. Peel had conceived the notion of a professional police force not only because it was long overdue, but also because that particular time, the late 1820s and early 1830s, was a perilous time to be alive. It was a time when the first real impact of mass immigration, extreme urban poverty, the crisis of radicalism and the challenges to the criminal justice system were all having a massive presence in both the metropolis and in the provinces. Riot and disorder had been common features across the land for the last eighty years and more were to follow in the 1830s. The previous system of runners and 'Charlies' (watchmen) had clearly been inefficient and prone to corruption.

Crime and the threat to social stability was noticeable everywhere. After all, in 1812 a British Prime Minister, Spencer Perceval, had been assassinated. In 1819 the massacre of Peterloo in Manchester had shown the ordinary people that the establishment was happy to set the army on them if they gathered for a meeting. London itself had 'no-go areas' in the rookeries where criminals could escape pursuit.

Detection was to come much later, long after the ruling mindset of prevention began to be seen as a failure. The law and its personnel in all areas had to learn that if detection could be established, however clumsily and slowly, then there might be a different kind of deterrent – something totally unlike the threat of beatings, imprisonment or transportation. As 'Plain clothes' was a detestable concept it also took a long time for something else to be recognised – the possibility that a police officer might be capable of understanding the villains by learning their cultural basis and their sense of social identity. The 'criminal tribe' was no longer to be a separate, inscrutable sub-group in its own circumscribed 'patches'.

This has been a quest for truth beneath the thick layering of myth and metaphor that has hidden the reality of this aspect of police history for so long. Beneath the literary and filmic imagery though, there has always been a desire on the part of artists and writers to reveal the untold story of the inner lives of detectives – the stuff of fiction that occasionally shows through the fabric of the course of social history.

My thanks go to the writers who previously applied their research and narrative expertise to this subject, notably Belton Cobb, Martin Fido, Keith Skinner and Douglas Browne. Staff at the London Metropolitan Archives have been very helpful and also my fellow crime writers Lesley Horton and John Styles.

ACKNOWLEDGEMENTS

Permission to use four pictures from the Metropolitan Police collection is accredited.

My thanks go to Eleanor Fletcher and Maggie Bird at the Resources Directorate.

Every effort has been made by staff at Getty Images and myself to trace the copyright for pictures from Percy Hoskins' book *No Hiding Place*. Four pictures from that book have been reproduced here, on the advice of professionals who helped with that search. Thanks also to the Alan Moss collection for the permission to reproduce the picture of Inspector Abiline, and to Essex Constabulary Police Museum.

BEFORE SCOTLAND YARD: AMATEURS AND LEARNERS

For centuries, ever since the first justices of the peace were established in the medieval period, the notion of acting against criminals was focused on the magistrate himself (at first voluntary) and the 'Reeve', later called the shire reeve and eventually 'Sheriff'. The system of criminal law before the mid-eighteenth century was largely concerned with accusers gathering and placing a recognizance before a local magistrate. He would then take action, but there were no officers to investigate.

In the tiny village of Long Riston, near Beverley, in 1799, a group of local people took out a recognizance against three people who they alleged had brutalised and eventually killed a little boy, the son of two of the accused. It was a case of murder. The adults clearly had the intention of beating and whipping the child until they had taken away his life. No one went out to start a process of enquiry and detection; they merely came to the East Riding of Yorkshire assizes to stand trial. Whatever investigation and evidence was collated there would be placed before the jury.

In that case, the assize records show something intriguing and fascinating. It is an occurrence that explains much of the local power and social interaction in criminal cases before the regional police forces slowly emerged after the Municipal Corporations Act of 1835. At the bottom of the assize record, written in pencil, are the words 'guilty' written next to all three accused. But then a line has been put through the name of the man. 'Not guilty' was written in its place. It would be a positive thought to assume that some kind of investigation

had taken place, but more likely we are talking about a local power structure: he may have had debts and transportation would have meant that these
debts would never have been recovered. He may simply have had powerful
friends. Or there may have been evidence to exonerate him.

British criminal history before the 1829 act, with the exception of those
parts of London around Bow Street, was subject to a dominance of the idea
of prevention, not detection. Cases of investigation and police work are rare
in the regions, while Henry Fielding and others, as we shall see, were beginning to establish detective work. There are rare examples, however, and one
case study from West Yorkshire shows that at times magistrates of special
ability did turn detective. Such a man was Samuel Lister, of Little Horton,
Bradford. Lister was living and working in the heartland of coiner country.
Clipping the King's coinage was a very lucrative business at that time (the
mid- to late-eighteenth century). Lister was a Justice of the Peace between
1751 and 1769, and he achieved a remarkable feat of detection – he tracked
down a forger to the source of his work and his base in Gloucestershire.

Coining then was a capital offence. The Calderdale coiners had made a
remote fastness in the hills to where they could retreat into farms well away
from the new towns. But Lister, along with his magistrate colleagues at the
time, was expected to take on a large workload and there was a shortage of
talented magistrates. By the last seven years of his period of office, a great
deal of the legal business of the western half of the textile areas around
Bradford came under his responsibility. One of his many duties, but one not
at all well defined, was to bring felons to justice. Most magistrates had no
time for this, but Lister went in pursuit of some, and his most outstanding
case was that of his detection of man who called himself Wilkins, apprehended for not paying his inn bill. In January 1756 Wilkins was standing in
the dock before Lister. The man had some highly unusual documentation
on him, including a letter from Lord Chedworth, giving him immunity
from arrest in a civil court. He also had a promissory note for the huge sum
of £1,100. Lister was intrigued.

It seemed that Wilkins had forged notes and bills, not actually clipped
coinage, but this was a capital offence. Lister did an amazing thing – he
circulated details of the man, notably into the area of Painswick, Gloucester.

He placed information in the London press also; the man was actually Edward Wilson, a clothier from Painswick. He had been forging bills in the West Country and was a wanted man. He was convicted and received a death sentence.

The kind of activity Lister engaged in was impossible for magistrates as a general rule; he was an outstanding man with a passion for detective work. What he did was almost a twentieth-century piece of police work, communicating across the counties to ascertain a true identity of a suspect. His suspect could have been released at any point on bail by a friend. There was therefore high drama: a chase for information before the system stopped both the arrest and the trial from taking place.

The general system of policing before Peel though, was one in which the key figures of magistrate, parish watch and other local dignitaries and landowners made up the general scene. In London, before Peel's act, we need to trace the beginnings of any smack of professionalism to the Fielding brothers: Henry the novelist, author of *Tom Jones*, and his blind brother John. Particularly after the beginnings of the gin craze, after its introduction into Britain in 1735, crime escalated in London and other towns. Assaults and robberies related to drunkenness, poverty, insanity and sheer desperation were subject to the brutal repression of the 'Bloody Code' – a long list of capital crimes on the statute books making such offences as stealing a sheep or even robbing a bit of cloth into a hanging matter.

In Fielding's London, the idea was that there would be a shift-work process, in which the good people of the city would take turns as constables. Of course, as they were unpaid and it was dangerous work, this did not happen. The small number of paid officers extended only to the 'Runners'. These existed in places other than Bow Street, but that location has claimed the name. At Bow Street the magistrates looked after the Runners and also the patrols. These were a small force of road patrol officers who policed the outskirts of the city. In central London the 'Charlies' were supposed to watch the streets in some areas, but they were subject to corruption and were not exactly fit men.

Dickens, writing in 1850, had another viewpoint on the Runners:

We are not by any means devout believers in the old Bow Street Police. To
say the truth, we think there was a vast amount of humbug about these wor-
thies. Apart from many of them being men of a very indifferent character,
and far too much in the habit of consorting with thieves … they never lost
a public occasion of jobbing and trading in mystery and making the most of
themselves …

Henry Fielding has to take the credit for the 'thief takers' however; he added
this small select group of men to the Bow Street staff after he became Chief
Magistrate at Bow Street in 1748. John Fielding, following him in 1754, was
really responsible for the larger force that became the Bow Street Runners.
Like Lister, however, Henry Fielding saw the importance of communication. He started the *Covent Garden Journal* in 1752. This only lasted for a
year, but it was far-sighted and was a beginning in this important branch of
detective work. A report in the issue for 10 March 1752, for instance, is the
first instance of the manoeuvre of 'putting a person up for identification'.
With details such as 'Saturday night last one Sarah Matthews, a woman of
near fourscore brought a woman of about twenty-four before Mr Fielding'
and 'It appeared that her former marriage was a falsehood and that the old
lady was the lawful wife … '

Of course, when there were severe riots, this force could not cope. When
there were major problems of social disorder, the army were called out; the
militias were accustomed to a tough repression in these cases. A common
solution to the problems of disorder was simply to intensify the military
actions, treating rioters as an enemy army. By the end of the eighteenth
century, when the country was quite used to large bodies of military
and naval men around the land, the militia regiments were often keen
to practise using swords and guns against the 'rabble'.

But something large scale and more humane was needed. The time was
right for a person with outstanding qualities of organisation and problem solving to appear. A man who had been Lord Provost of Glasgow,
Patrick Colquhoun, was that man. After moving south to London in 1789,
he became a magistrate. He was only thirty-seven but eager to achieve

something substantial in this context. His concept was that it was high time that something more than mere prevention of crime was needed. His book *A Treatise on the Police of the Metropolis*, published in 1796, went through seven editions in ten years. Colquhoun was many things, including the father of the soup kitchen, a result of his profound concern for the plight of the poor. He was one of those philanthropists who were also known at the time as commercial diplomats – a product of the Enlightenment who noticed the underclass and cared about them.

Colquhoun had the vision to see that what was needed was a number of police commissioners, men with salaries and defined responsibilities. He even suggested a place in the proposed new order for the watchmen, advocating them as a reserve force as the militia is to the regular army. The platform for opposition to his ideas would come from the rates, the ongoing problem of why the British rate-payers would want to finance men in a 'police state' in which the notion of law would be revolutionised and the ordinary man deprived of personal liberties. Colquhoun saw that some duties second-ary to actual crime prevention could be included in the remit of the hypothetical police force. Obviously, Robert Peel was aware of these ideas and they were undoubtedly an influence on his thinking a few decades later.

He also conceived of a series of districts with departmental officers, something that would happen in 1829. But he was more than a crime theorist. Colquhoun was also a statistician and a typically enthusiastic social scientist of his age, gathering facts and figures, listing businesses and traders in various categories. All this would play a part in his thinking as he devised what we would now call the application of logistics to the municipal corporations' functioning. As he wrote, the cost of policing would, 'go very far towards easing the resources of the County of the expenses of what the Select Committee of the House of Commons denominate a very inefficient system of police.'

Pitt, in 1798, forwarded these ideas to Parliament but there was a massive and widespread protest. When a bill developed from these pro-posals was about to be discussed in the chamber, Pitt stood down. The consequences of this led to the bill being dropped. But there was one aspect that survived and was applied, and it was a very important one – the policing of the docks. As the new police were to discover in the 1830s, trying to tackle the problems of smuggling and theft along the Thames was a gargantuan problem and it was open to corruptive practises. At times, constables in Peel's force were to be subject to the temptation of co-operation with the villains, such were the financial rewards available. Colquhoun wrote about the 'plundering' of the docklands. He saw the weaknesses in the process of revenue investigation and excise, and he proposed a river police. By 26 June 1798, it was announced that a river police to be called the Marine Police Institution was to be formed immediately, with its base at Wapping. It was a force of considerable presence, having eighty officers in its original staff. This came about because of a Captain Harriott, who was a magistrate as well as a navy man. Then in 1800, a bill was passed (with the help of Jeremy Bentham) to provide the Thames Police Office with three stipendiary magistrates. Harriott himself took control of this for six years.

It has to be asked what detective work was being done, if any, in the early decades of the nineteenth century before Peel's act. Historians have traditionally studied this by means of looking at the massive and sensational crimes of those years, from the Ratcliffe Highway murders of 1811 to the case of the body snatchers and 'The Italian Boy' horrors of 1831. There is no doubt that such cases highlighted the nature of detective work and also hinted at what kind of expertise was needed to improve. Add to these the murder cases involving Daniel Good and the butler Courvoisier in 1840–1 and we have several good reasons why the call for a detective force was made.

The Ratcliffe Highway murders of 1811 concerned the household of a draper called Timothy Marr on this road going east from London, running through some of the worst areas of the city for crime. A maid discovered Marr, together with his wife and baby, murdered. But they were killed in such messy, brutal and bloody ways that it was a sensational affair. The baby in its cot had had its throat cut and its skull battered. The investigation pinpointed the shortcomings of the available police forces, because the Thames Police, the Shadwell magistrates and the local churchwardens had all failed to achieve anything in spite of arresting several people. At that time a man could be arrested simply because someone saw him near the scene of crime.

There were sightings and details of the actual killer, or killers, including a man called Turner who gave a description of a tall man wearing a specific style of coat. But, as with every high-profile murder that is not seemingly for profit or plunder, the doors were open for hysteria and myth-making. Even the famous writer Thomas de Quincey took hold of the case as a way of writing about meaningless killing, linked to a very modern notion of the sociopath.

It was the magistrates who were having to play detective and they had two suspects, Williams and Peterson, each with bloodied clothing and with visits to a public house under observation. But Williams hanged himself in a cell and from that point it was assumed that he was the killer. This case made it clear to the people of London that there was a case for the establishment of a police force. The estimated cost of such a force was put at £74,000 and the notion was forgotten. In terms of attempts at detection though, it had been an abject failure, pinpointing the abysmal lack of procedure, common sense and most of all co-ordination in the forces of law.

Taking a wider picture, this was a bad time for England – we were almost certainly about to go to war with America and the war in France was going badly. There were Luddite troubles in the North and various dignitaries were causing a stir about the inhumane criminal justice system and the disgusting state of the prisons and local gaols. With hindsight, it is a simple matter to see that another reason for a police force, particularly at that period, was to take some of the strain on men and resources put on the armed forces. There had been a standing army in the North and Midlands for many decades, ready to deal with radicals and riots. Soldiers were based in most main Yorkshire towns, for instance, ready to assemble in trouble hot-spots at any time. As late as the mid-1830s, under Feargus O'Connor, the 'Physical Force' Chartists were drilling with weapons on Woodhouse Moor, in Leeds. Nothing provides a sharper contrast between the French and British ideologies of criminal law and the morality of policing than the gap between the French detective in the system and the British. Before the reforms of Fouché in France, there had always been the 'King's Police' and these had contained *agents provocateurs.* The *Ancien Regime* in France had established the idea of police as an integral element of the espionage functions of legal controls on the populace.

Joseph Fouché took over the French Ministry of Police in 1799 when the old tradition of detective work being espionage was carried on. Fouche recruited three hundred officers to use as spies; when Vidocq took over the *Brigade de Sureté* he was a part of Fouche's organisation, something that worked organically, with excellent communications between different *arondissements* in Paris. As James Morton has pointed out, Britain did not monitor this: 'It is both curious and alarming that, more than seventy years later, the Metropolitan Police had still not learned from Vidocq and the French.' Early on in the British new police, there were several instances of the consequences of this lack of united work across the London areas. Frederick Wensley, who wrote a memoir, *Detective Days* (1931) and who joined the police as late as 1888 still noted that there were weaknesses in this respect: 'When I joined, an officer, except by definite instructions, was scarcely ever permitted to go outside his own division. The result was that criminals living in one district could, almost with impunity, commit crimes in another.'

But before 1829, the detectives that existed were either Bow Street patrolmen or sheer amateurs. That is, if we count *agents provocateurs* in industrial protest as separate beings. The most interesting glimpse we have of these men is in the writings of the radical leaders. The reference here is to spies and informers, but there is no doubt that what these men and their superiors learned in the decades of working class unrest and political sedition, where the establishment looked with fear across at the French Revolution, was an integral part of later detective practice. How else could any idea of what plain clothes work meant possibly be gained in the ordinary course of life? The fears of the forces of law and authority had been extreme; in 1817 the Habeas Corpus Suspension Act and the Seditious Meetings Act made it very easy for a magistrate to have anyone dragged to court who was present at a political gathering of any kind. In that way, the radicals and reformists were pushed underground, hence the need for spies and informers.

One of the best sources we have in explanation of this paranoid atmosphere is in the memoirs of Samuel Bamford, the Lancastrian radical leader.

In his book *Passages in the Life of a Radical*, he defines the nature of this focus of unease and suspicion at the time: 'Our unity of action was relaxed … plans were broached quite different from any that had been recognised by the Hampden Clubs; and the people, at a loss to distinguish friends from enemies, were soon prepared for the operation of informers … '

A clear instance of this infiltration of radical workers can be found in the history of Bradford Chartism. In 1839/40, when the Chartism forces in the West Riding were gathering for trouble and actually buying fire-arms and drilling, the government agents came north, stealthily – plain clothes men selected by the Home Secretary's associates for a hard task. In 1839, the vast open space of Peep Green near Bradford (now known as Hartshead Moor) was the scene of a massive Chartist rally. The area was like a fair, with huts put up for the sale of food and drink. Some accounts say that half a million people were there, but 200,000 is probably closer to the mark. O'Connor was there, speaking to the masses; it was, for some present, the preparation for a bloody confrontation with the forces of law and order. At the time, there was no provincial police force at all, though police officers did come north at times to help in difficult cases and special circumstances.

A leader called Bussey was keen to have an armed body of men march-ing on Bradford, and some followed him. Shopkeepers had had visits from desperate men eager to use rifles against the soldiers who would inevitably arrive. William Egan, a Bradford gunsmith, recalled how he had had visits from locals asking if he had guns or bayonets in stock. He said that he had not. In this atmosphere the agents arrived, and one of these was a certain James Harrison. In December 1839 he gave an account of what was going on with the extremists. He had been to a meeting at the Queen's Head tavern, four miles from Bradford, and there he had heard that there were 260 men armed and ready to strike. There was also a London Chartist at this meeting and Harrison must have been worried. He recalled that there was a delegate in the bar called George Flinn. Another Londoner looked earnestly at Flinn and asked if he knew Harrison. Flinn, Harrison recalled, 'Had known me for three years and said I was as good as any man in the room … ' Nevertheless, that was a tense moment.

With hindsight it is clear that when the call for a detective department came, administrators and statesmen, civil servants and army types, all began to realise that the espionage in the Napoleonic wars, agent-spies in the turbulent radical provinces, and Bow Street men in the metropolis, all had experience of what would become arguably the most dramatic aspect of detective activities. When the new police arrived, the 'plain clothes' element was the one attracting the most suspicion and criticism. In 1830, one Sergeant Tyrell arrested some thieves in the Strand and a Bow Street magistrate noted, 'I don't suppose he ever would have detected them if he had worn his uniform.' It was common practice to have some officers wearing what were then called 'coloured clothes ' on duty – to all effects and purposes detectives.

The period before the 1829 Act was, then, one dominated by the repercussions of European war and radical unrest at home. As the massive spillage of poverty and petty crime hit London and other towns at this time, it became clear that the watchmen and the few magistrates could not cope. The Fieldings and Colquhoun, along with some prominent Bow Street Runners, contributed a great deal in terms of organisation and efficiency, but only on a small scale.

In spite of their reputation for inefficiency, the Runners provided several instances of good detective work and they remained a limited presence throughout the years of the new police, until some of the Runners were assimilated into the first detective force. For instance, the famous murderer of Maria Marten – Corder – was arrested by Lea, the Runner from Lambeth. But there were only half a dozen Runners and the method of work was like that of a freelancer, paid by the person or organisation that had called on them.

The Runners were fundamentally for hire and found their work extremely lucrative. The group of Runners took their share in the money distributed among any group of witnesses who had played a part in a conviction for a felony; they averaged £20 a year from this. In addition, they received items called Tyburn tickets. These were exemption tickets from more onerous work as a constable across the city; they were valuable and made around £20 when sold. One of the best-known Runners, Townsend, along with some colleagues, managed to operate as a special security unit, guarding royalty, opera houses and clubs. After George III had been attacked as he stepped down from his coach in St James's Palace in 1786, a woman called Margaret Nicholson came forward and made a lunge at the King's chest with a knife. The King played this down and showed some understanding sympathy for her, saying she was 'mad'. But after that, what we would now call special duties by detectives – guarding the sovereign – were undertaken by Townsend. He received a huge sum of £200 a year for these special duties, and Townsend became very popular with the King.

Yet the Runners did establish many of the common practices of later professional detectives in their methods of work. Their visits to 'flash houses' for instance, in which they cultivated their informers, were essential to their limited success. They learned, by trial and error, to create a range of good information sources and to have a few key contacts for immediate reference when anything of major importance happened, such as a kidnapping or a high-profile robbery.

In previous historical writing on the period before Peel's revolution, detectives had perhaps been overshadowed by the tales of sensational thefts and murders, events that usually take centre stage in the chronicles of crime. But the amateurs were there, and some limited inroads had been made into those practices that would become essential as the new police began to see the need for a detective department.

PEEL, MAYNE AND ROWAN

In the 1820s, Sir Robert Peel distinguished himself in so many areas of reform that is it not difficult to make him the epitome of that particular variety of zeal embodied in the northerner who extends the hard work ethos of manufacture into the world of planning. From the year 1822 when he became home secretary in Liverpool's government, he was busy with several areas of the penal and criminal justice systems, as well as becoming Tory 'man of the moment' in the debate over Catholic Emancipation, moving from opponent to statute creator in a later guise in Wellington's government. Peel not only conceived of the new police force: he began a long-overdue process of sorting out the parlous state of the local gaols across the land. In addition, he made the first Prisons Act of 1823 the first stage in a major overhaul of the penal system. Over 100 capital offences were abolished. This act, along with the 1824 Prison Discipline Act, created regulatory measures for local prisons, mainly forcing inspections by magistrates. The year after that he instituted Home Office inspectors.

Philanthropists and amateur documentarists such as John Howard had looked closely at the nation's gaols over the last sixty years, with Howard as the first man there with his monumental *The State of the Prisons* (1771). But throughout the first decade of the new century *The Gentleman's Magazine* had conducted its own survey from Newcastle to Devon, and all this information played a part in helping Peel understand the practical implementation of punishment within the justice system. From these first studies of prisons and offences, Peel began to see where the deficiencies lay overall. He had no need to be reminded of the evidence of criminal activity around him as he read the reports. At the time he became home secretary there were riots in Frome and in Warminster over the use of a new shuttle, and there was violence at a colliers' strike in Wales. In Norwich and in Newcastle that year (1822) there were confrontations between masters and men and again, the army were needed.

With regard to a police force, Peel wasted no time in getting to work. One of his first Select Committees resulted in a small step forward – head constables were appointed for each of the eight police offices across London that had been there since 1792. There was also a daily patrol established and the issue of the uniform was discussed again. Suggestions of militarism caused panic and protest in all quarters. This new patrol wore the red and blue of the horse patrol. Peel was full of ideas, seeming to want to accelerate change in several areas at once. He even had plans to rebuild the Bow Street office and to design routes for the patrols in accordance with the demographic profile of a specific location.

By 1826 he had the desk clear ready to consider the creation of a professional police force in London. This was not entirely a concept made *ex nihilo*. As the Irish troubles had continued, notably after the Wolfe Tone rebellion of 1797, a constabulary had been established in Ireland. An act of 1814 had created what was called a Peace Preservation Force there, and in 1822, as Peel came into office, a proper training school had been made for the Irish constables. He turned his attention to London with the Dublin template in mind; all he stayed clear of was the city square mile. In the history of detective staff, that was to be crucially important, as the City of London Police and the Metropolitan notably developed with communication issues. But by 1828 Peel was back in power after a lull, this time in Wellington's government, and as Wellington loved the notion of a regiment and the sense of control and purpose inherent in that, Peel had something to go on when he developed his arguments. Wellington sensed that the city urgently needed either an army present or a police force. Peel was just the man to give him the latter. It was simply a matter of moving quickly to yet another Select Committee stage and then things could happen.

At the core of the mess he sought to deal with were the watch system and the proliferation of parish officials. His concept was simple – scrap the parish with its eighteen different local Boards each acting without concert with the others, and replace it with one central body for law and order. In his speech explaining the bill he said, 'My Bill enables the Secretary of State to abolish gradually the existing Watch establishments, to substitute in their room a police force that shall act by night and day … I propose to substitute a new police for the old one, not to attempt too much at first … ' Peel knew that progress would be slow, but that small steps reached the goal. His experience as Secretary of State for Ireland and the Irish constabulary had taught him that.

We have to go deeper into the social fabric of the age to understand the complexity of the introduction of a police force as a preventative element. Clearly crime is in some way always related to poverty and deprivation. Desperate people will slip into criminal ways. One detective, the famous Jerome Caminada from Manchester, explains this very well in his casebook when he talks about the few families in the slums who were for a time clear of crime, but then:

> … they were up against fearful odds, as they came into daily contact with professional thieves and fallen women, who you would often see parading in Market Street … I have seen such apparently decent families begin to lose, and then lose completely, all respectability, as penniless and unable to get food they slipped into the first layers of crime and gradually sank into the abyss.

As in all societies at all times, the categories of criminals divide into those who break the law from desperation and necessity and those who think of crime as their career. Peel knew very well what the main causes of both categories of crime were. To understand the patterns and nature of crime in London at the time, we need to recall the need for instruments of law to include the human narratives within the criminal casebook.

A clear way to see the surface of this crime, through the eyes of a police constable, is to note what was reflected in the new *Police Gazette* or *Hue and Cry* as it was sub-titled. A typical issue contained a list of deserters from His Majesty's Service; accounts of murder, arson, house-breaking, horse and cattle stealing, larceny, frauds and aggravated misdemeanours. Stolen property is listed and lists of people charged are given for each office: Bow Street, Queen Square, Marlborough, Marylebone, Hatton Garden, Worship Street, Lambeth Street, Thames Police and Union Hall. It is plain to see that the accounts of events have exactly the same mix of detail and common sense that Fielding had in his journal, and the lines of thought that detectives adopt are delineated, as seen in issue 190 of the *Gazette*:

> On Saturday afternoon, the 7th instant, about a quarter before three o'clock, a man, about five feet five inches high, dressed in a blue coat, a light striped waistcoat, black trousers, white cravat, black hat and pea-green kid gloves, of sallow complexion, and rather high cheekbones, went to the house of Henry Elphick … in company with a man … They had something to drink, And when the first named man gave the landlady a half sovereign and ten Shillings, and requested her to give him a sovereign for them. She went to the further bar for that purpose and while there he took from the table a leather bag and took out of it twelve sovereigns and a half, with which they both walked away.

That was going to be the bread-and-butter work, then – thousands of everyday thefts and assaults. But within that mass of people there were undoubtedly many who were once good citizens but who had been brutalised, such as the deserters who had fought abroad, been flogged and half-starved and ended up rootless and open to being suborned into crime.

Peel needed a system that would allow for the massive range of crimes of varying degrees of heinous or intolerable consequences; he needed men in the ranks who would not only act in a military fashion but who would learn to match their knowledge of the law with their knowledge of human nature. When the first men went out onto the beats, it soon became obvious that there was going to be major crime in with the minor crime. The nature of that more serious crime was to introduce the need for a detective force. But Peel's first concerns in 1830 were about who would be his new commissioners. In May 1829, Sir George Murray, one of Wellington's top men in his Peninsular campaign, wrote to Charles Rowan to let him know that his name was being put before Peel as a contender for the forthcoming post of Police Commissioner. Like so many great leaders and organisers of the Victorian military and empire structures, Rowan was an Ulsterman. He had come to Wellington's notice commanding the 52nd Foot Regiment and had commanded a wing at Waterloo, where he was wounded. Rowan retired from the army in 1822. What must have impressed Peel was the fact that Rowan had started with that regiment as an ensign in 1797 and stayed with them, being paymaster along the way.

Much has been made of the links between Rowan's past military experience and the imprint of discipline and behaviour he made on the new constabulary. For instance, it has been noted that he learned the 'Shorncliffe system' of using liaising bands of skirmishes from Sir John Moore – this was a method of having protection for a group of men at the front and rear. As the police had to be military in action as well as in presence and dress, this tactic would be used on the streets of London when needed, just as it had been used in war. There is much substance in this – Rowan came from a place of innovation. Shorncliffe Camp was where Moore trained his light division, and it was at that same place that Colonel Shrapnel had invented his spherical case shot. There would certainly be situations in which officers were outnumbered and in which they had to deal with aggressive crowds who were prepared to attack them, as in industrial disorder or in food riots.

It was because Rowan had 'brought his regiment to the highest state of discipline' (Wellington's words) that he was offered the post of Metropolitan Police Magistrate. He accepted. But Peel knew from the start that such a massive undertaking required two men, each with different abilities and attitudes. Rowan would provide the structure and order, the career status and *esprit de corps*. Peel found a young lawyer with experience of work on the Northern Circuit, Richard Mayne, to be the counterbalance to Rowan. A theorist was needed, but also someone who knew the law from the grass roots, a man who saw how people's everyday lives impinged on the criminal justice system. He could also be essential in the valuable art of writing documents, instructions and commands, and one of the first duties of the new commissioners was to draft a set of guidelines for practice.

Rowan could see the need for a set of divisions, with groups of men in equivalent portions to those of regiment, platoon and company. Even the idea of a beat was a military concept, based on patrol and surveillance. But at the core of all the new police work had to be a book of rules. Rowan and Mayne set to work on what would become the General Instructions. Rowan wrote most of the material on conduct, professional standards and discipline; Mayne was handy with the couching of words in very particular ways and contexts. It has to be said, although it has little to do with Mayne's character, that Peel could not really afford a salary that would have attracted a celebrated lawyer. But he was to instil the notion of promotion 'from the bottom up' right from the start of the force. Mayne was one of the sons of the judges of the Court of King's Bench in Dublin. At twenty-two he took his B.A. at Trinity, then the B.A. and Master's at Cambridge. When he started his new job for Peel he was just thirty three – fourteen years younger than Rowan.

Mayne's friend Lawrence Peel (no relation to the Home Secretary) advised the young lawyer to apply for the new post in the city, and with Mayne eager to marry the daughter of a Mr Carvick, he was in need of a decent income. The commissioner post would bring him £800 a year – a very handsome sum. Yet the whole business of Richard Mayne taking this post is highly unusual, as previous writers have pointed out. For instance, Mayne was never interviewed. In addition to that, Mayne did not meet his partner until after he was appointed. In today's world of teamwork, liaison and joint management planning, this appears very odd indeed. Would they be able to work together? It must have crossed the minds of the civil servants around Peel at the time. Clearly, Mayne had intellectual powers and a sound command of language. But Peel must have seen more in the young man's record than that.

It seems that Mayne, the active lawyer used to planning for the court process and the interplay of defence and prosecution, would naturally be a careful schemer, a man of logic as well as imagination, whereas Rowan would be inured to adapting to events. Despite his being accustomed to moving and participating in a world of pragmatism and whimsicality, he must have been surprised at Peel's behaviour. Of this he wrote, 'I saw him on Monday, at his house, when he said he was going to appoint two persons to organize and direct the new police, that he had sent for me to offer one of the places to me, that if the place suited my views he was happy to offer it.' He had been located and appraised initially by a number of men in the judiciary, as under-secretary at the Home Office, William Gregson, had written in 1829. Mayne then met Rowan in Peel's office, on 6 July, and Mayne accepted the post and salary. The new police could now step into history.

It would have been likely, had anyone provided an estimation of how the new partnership would progress, that the young lawyer would have quickly been overshadowed by the old soldier. But sources indicate that Rowan was very open-minded and considerate with regard to Mayne. There was to be a difference of perspective though, which concerned the difference between a military view of the individual within a system and the more liberal civilian Regency middle class view. In short, where Rowan would shout and threaten, Mayne would suggest encouragement and offer inducements to greater enthusiasm for the job. A large proportion of the new constables were sacked in the first few years, mostly because of drunkenness. They were going to be subject to the same inducements and corruptive practices as the Runners, of course.

The differing concepts of the status and nature of police work is reflected in the two men's contributions to the *General Instructions*. Rowan saw the possibilities for men being pushed into breaking 'regulations' whenever inducements such as awards and rewards were mentioned by Mayne. The interplay of the two voices provides a plain statement of the continuing dichotomy of the police officer's uneasy situation with regard to the new profession in the first decades of the force. On 29 September 1829, the birth of the Metropolitan Police took place. The officers paraded in the grounds of the Foundling Hospital and it was a typical regimental drill, except for one small detail – a few of the men arrived the worse for drink. Peel was destined to have his name imprinted in various forms on his progeny; being accused not only of having a 'private army' but of having a mass of 'Peelers' and 'Bobbies'. The two latter terms, together with 'Peel's Raw Lobsters' were derogatory, but over time, of course, there was a grudging respect attached. The real substance of Peel's thought about the self-identity of the force was not only the notion of ranks being 'filled from below' but that he was deeply against any individual feeling superior to another. In essence, what he had done in 1829 was make one force of men to patrol an area covering a seven-mile radius from Charing Cross, with six divisions and each division with its stipendiary magistrate.

It was surely a huge and public vindication of this establishment when in 1831 a huge crowd attacked the Duke of Wellington's home at Apsley House on Hyde Park, breaking all the windows, and the police restored order.

Before the first official detective department, major cases of murder and similarly high profile offences were so demanding that they demanded detective work, and a number of prominent individuals made names for themselves in the decade before the landmark 1842 arrival of detectives as a recognised arm of the police. The cases that highlighted these prototype sleuths are important ones in the history of homicide. These men had a special, rather wayward and dashing role in the ranks of the police; they had a roving task, a free hand to intervene and to add other skills to those of their uniformed colleagues, though only in their own divisions – with the exception of the remarkable Nicholas Pearce. Pearce was an ex-sergeant and ex-Runner working in 1830 in the docklands area. But his talents were soon recognised and used – he was a detective deep in his nature, a man with strong powers of observation and attention to detail. The question is how did the detectives fit into the new police in this first decade before they officially existed as staff with offices and locations?

The answer is that, like Pearce, they appear to have been able to act when and if there were special circumstances. Naturally, this happened because the uniformed police had limitations and deficiencies. After all, they had to concentrate on dealing with petty crime, public relations, maintaining their image and cultivating intensive local knowledge. All that made for a very full week's work, without any Holmesian deduction and study of abstruse forensics. But a turning point came in the Popay case in 1833 when the plain clothes man was found out, making the commissioners reluctant to admit that there were plain clothes activities. However, a statement in *Police Orders* for 26 April 1837 refers to some officers used to maintain order at a royal event. The list comprises '44 plain clothes men' as well as ordinary constables. As time went on in the 1830s, it became increasingly necessary to use plain clothes. There was a jewel robbery at Welbeck in 1840 and instructions were given in *Police Orders* for 'an active intelligent man in each division' to be assigned to searching out the missing jewels. That is a clear indication of the incipient detective branch. *Police Orders* were regular instructions and guidance, at first handwritten but later printed. They were at first concerned with the ad hoc actions and reactions involved in crime fighting but later they included professional and career information.

Another reason why the detective force was creeping in was that from the very first month of the new police, the constables themselves were vulnerable to attack, and murders were too common for comfort. The first officer killed was P.C. Grantham in Euston. Robert Culley was killed at the Cold Bath Fields Riot in 1832, just off Gray's Inn Road. In an event that highlights the deficiencies of the detective thinking of 1830, P.C. Long was stabbed to death also on Gray's Inn Road, and the policeman involved, Inspector Busalin, arrested anyone sitting nearby and eventually hanged a man on slim evidence, mainly based on the fact that he was wearing a brown coat. In 1830, John Busalin of G Division, centred on the King's Cross station, knew only one essential challenge after the murder of his constable – that a man must be arrested and hanged for the offence. He knew that three men had run from the murder scene and that an old woman had at first said she witnessed the killing and that one man had a brown coat. Only one man apprehended had a brown coat – a man who called himself Smith. When he turned out to be another man with another name, it was enough for a conviction. William Sapwell did indeed hang for the murder. There was no sound evidence against him at all.

It seems incredible now, but police at that time knew nothing about the necessity to gather relevant and important evidence. The spirit of hue and cry was still in the air, and indeed Busalin raised the hue and cry in this case.

Hearsay, distorted information, individual reputation and circumstantial details – all these played a part in the process of detection. The mindset was one of crime prevention, so the complicated business of the detection of the guilty party was a secondary thing. As long as there was an arrest, most parties in the affair were happy.

Sir Robert Peel had his commissioners, then; the country had its first professional police force, and they had quickly been called to action. Rowan's role was never in doubt, but Mayne was to have his reputation assured as time went on and he matured as a professional man very quickly, such was his huge responsibility in the new office.

The commissioners and the police structure were never too far away from life to be free from satire and ridicule though, as their business was centred on human life on the streets, in the markets and in the clubs and pubs. *The Times*, for instance, had fun just two days before the first drill in the Foundling Hospital. They spotted a discrepancy in that the *General Instructions* was a massive tome while police constables had been chosen for their frames and fists rather than for their grey matter:

> Mr Secretary Peel must have laughed at some parts of that volume which
> has been prepared for the edification and guidance of the new police. If their
> recruits can understand, or even read it through in a year, they will certainly
> be very different from their thief-taking or thief-screening predecessors …
>
> (*The Times* 27 September, 1829)

3

THE FIRST DECADES:
THE SOCIAL HISTORY OF
THE NEW DETECTIVES

The detective branch was eventually formed in 1842 after a succession of murder cases which had highlighted the deficiencies of the plain utilitarian organisation of the military-minded preventative uniformed men. The reason why the detective work going on before the official establishment was so hated was that it reflected the continental model from Fouché. In England, naturally, when undercover methods were used they were done against the working classes. Bearing in mind that the expanding middle class thought all crime came from the 'underclass' and the 'working men in drink', this was acceptable.

From the beginning, the detective was caught between the hands-on work amongst his criminal fraternity on his 'patch' and the strict code of conduct written down for him to follow in the rulebook. But he was a figure increasingly needed as the decade 1830–40 wore on and sensational crimes made it plain that something more than a constable with a notebook and truncheon was needed. Two cases in particular illustrate this: the murder of Lord William Russell by his butler in May 1840; and the pursuit of the killer Daniel Good in April 1842. These two cases very clearly pointed to the shortcomings of the current preventative system and the lack of specialists.

The Russell murder was certain to make the headlines and to cause panic in the ranks of the aristocracy. Lord William Russell was an elderly widower living close to Park Lane. He had been an art connoisseur and a family man, not a player in government, but he was the brother of the Duke of Bedford. When two constables heard a commotion near Russell's house in May 1840 a series of events was to unfold that tested the deductive skills of the more acute officers.

The constables went to the Russell house, and there they found the butler weeping and upstairs was the body of Lord Russell, the throat cut, lying on the bed. First, the scene was fully studied by Inspector Tedman of C Division, but Inspector Beresford (the man in that division) came later to take control. After that, a mass of people was to arrive, including Mayne himself. The murder of such a notable person was very rare indeed. There would have to be a careful examination of the scene, and in fact there was much to observe.

On the surface, this appeared to be a burglary in which the old lord had disturbed the robber – a maid had found some valuables on the floor near a door and other valuable items were known to have gone missing. The butler, Courvoisier, was a Swiss who had not long been in Russell's service. Searching through all the servants' possessions, Beresford found a chisel in Courvoisier's bag. This matched the marks made on some drawers that had been forced open. There was no doubt who was the major suspect then. By this time, Nicholas Pearce had joined the detectives. He was the former Bow Street Runner who had already made a good reputation working on several earlier cases. He was part of A Division – by that time the elite corps of the Metropolitan Police. Pearce and Beresford did some impressive deductive thinking with regard to the burning-down time for the rush light in a shade that was used as the aristocrat's reading light. Relating the doctor's estimated time of death for the old man to the burning of the light, it was seen that the light was put out at the time of the killing.

There were several suspects, and Courvoisier was the likely villain, but there were no items from the stolen property to hand. They had to be somewhere in the house and officers kept a close watch on the Swiss. Time went on and the newspapers were restless. Expecting the detectives to be a noted improvement on the old Runners, they were quick to criticise them when no developments occurred. It was even suggested that the detectives in the new police were nowhere near as skilled and full of local savvy as the old officers. But the team was in the house, searching meticulously for the stolen objects. It is notable that the two men brought in had been impressive in searches in other cases, and that they were not ignorant of the fact that the servant was nervous when they were in his quarters.

Nicholas Pearce was the man who saw the telling detail – a skirting board with some freshly disturbed plaster. On being forced open, the panel revealed a hole in which there was a cache of coins and a medal from Waterloo. Courvoisier was charged and arrested. He appeared at the Old Bailey and the continuing high profile case prompted *The Times* to elaborate on its suggestions for a detective force. It had taken an attack on one of the lords of the land to create a demand for something closer to the continental system. If we were going to be killed in our beds, then something should be done other than collar drunkards in the streets, the argument ran; we should have men out there, an elite of detectives to know where the desperate men like this Swiss villain were living and planning their vile deeds.

A long letter in *The Times* outlined an idea to mix the best of the old Runners with a new elite force, and that this should be a detective branch. The dreaded phrase 'plain clothes' was used. Suddenly, that was not so terrifying a thought, not now that killers were infiltrating Mayfair. The police were on trial as well as Courvoisier that week at the Old Bailey. Although there were criticisms, mainly due to the reward offered for the capture of the killer, it must have been impressive to see Pearce bring a carpenter into court with a model door and doorpost simply to show that some hammer-marks matched the ones noted at the scene. The defence tried to use the reward as an element of their argument, raising the issue whenever they could, but as the trial went on, some of the missing spoons turned up, brought by a French woman named Piolaine. It was all up for Courvoisier, who was sentenced to death. In his last speech he admitted that Lord Russell had disturbed him during a mock burglary.

The case was significant in that it shed light for the reading public on what went on in the police procedure in a murder case. The road was open for anyone to play detective and have a theory on what actually happened that night in Norfolk Street, Park Lane, and what sort of mind the evil Swiss valet had and why that was so. It made detective work not only visible but open to public participation, albeit vicariously.

The Daniel Good case made something else visible – the consequences of not having co-ordination across the divisions. The affair began when a constable was called to a pawnbroker's in Wandsworth, where some items had been stolen and the pawnbroker knew that the thief was Daniel Good, a coachman. Constable Gardner traced Good to the stables where he was based and, sensibly, began a search of the premises. The constable found a human torso in the straw, and he was horrified when Good ran and locked him in the stables. The policeman had lost his suspect. The first response would have boded well for a speedy capture of the escapee, because in the morning all the police stations in the London area knew about the man and the escape. What happened then was a farcical failure to use the information and the advantage of quick communication.

The system in use was the route paper, which meant that the inspector in the office where a crime had occurred wrote details and gave these to a reserve officer to be a courier to the next division, and this was repeated until all parties had been informed. Each receipt was initialled. Copies also went to sergeants leading the beat patrols. They were all centrally checked so that the operation of the system could be monitored. On this occasion, they were not quick enough to keep up with Good. At the end of the chain of communications was one of Good's former wives, Molly, and it seems as though Good would have been caught there (in Spitalfields) had it not been for the too obvious and public arrival of the officer intending to arrest him.

The result of all this was that Good eluded capture and disappeared. Pearce was brought in and he sensibly traced all the women who would be likely to be attractions for the runaway, and he also thought of checking docks in case the man was thinking of going overseas. But in the end it was good luck not good management that led to the capture of Daniel Good. A former policeman called Rose saw Good working at Tonbridge one day and he was caught, tried and hanged. He had murdered his woman, Jane Sparks.

The Good case had shown the limitations of the route paper system; it made it clear that something else was needed – something relying on the kind of expertise that comes with intimate knowledge of location and demography. The detective branch was about to be born.

The plain clothes branch was formed at Scotland Yard on 15 August 1842. It was headed by Nicholas Pearce with John Haynes as deputy. The other six men were Stephen Thornton, William Gerrett, Frederick Shaw, Charles Goff, Jonathan Whicher and Sergeant Braddick. Rowan and Mayne had sent a memo to the Home Secretary on 'the detective powers of the police'. Their first detectives were a mixed bunch but their varied experience was a significant advantage to them in their future work together. Haynes, for instance, was a chemist and Goff had come through the ranks. The new outfit was to be known simply as 'The Detective'. It was only, in one sense, a rationalisation of a pattern that had been slowly emerging – Metropolitan Police had been sent out on special missions to the provinces sometimes, to help with intractable problems of detection, such as the journey to Uxbridge of Sergeant Otway in 1837. Otway and Pearce had become a regular team in such adventures.

There was another reason why a detective force was a needful initiative – the supervision and investigation of the police themselves. This was to be made apparent in the complex case of the murder of P.C. Clark at Dagenham in 1846. Clark had gone missing on his country beat and a wealth of suspects were assembled after his body was found brutally murdered in a field. But part of that picture was the possibility that police officers had been working a scam with some Thames smugglers and ship-robbers. During the course of the investigations into Clark's death, it became clear that groups of officers in remote areas could wield a great deal of local power, and that could easily corrupt.

But 'The Detective' had arrived and the phenomenon drew the attention of the public and the media. One man who saw the allure of the detective's life and character was Charles Dickens. Not only did Dickens invent the first substantial characterisation of a detective in English literature (Inspector Bucket in *Bleak House*) he also wrote thousands of words in non-fictional genres to give his public a relish for this new breed of men.

In his *Uncommercial Traveller* sketches he went out for a night with the Liverpool police, but in 'The Modern Science of Thief-Taking', written for the periodical *Household Words* in July 1850, he begins to use his knowledge of the new men in print. He met Jonathan Whicher and calls him 'Whichem' in various essays. Dickens understood the spirit of the human nexus in the nature of thief-taking. That is, relationships have to be forged across the line, into the no-man's-land between the established police practice and the risk-taking double-identity of this 'new science':

> In order to counteract the plans of the swell mob, two of the sergeants of the detective police make it their business to know every one of them personally. The consequence is, that the appearance of either of these officers upon any scene of operations is a bar to anything or anybody being 'done'. This is an excellent characteristic of the detective, for they thus become as well a Preventive Police.

There is more than this in what Dickens understood, however. As a man who knew the physical materiality of London from his interminable nocturnal rambles, he saw the new crimes and instinctively sensed their subtlety:

> But the tricks and contrivances of those who wheedle money out of your pocket rather than steal it; who cheat you with eyes open; who clear every vestige of plate out of your pantry while your servant is on the stairs ... for the detection and punishment of such impostors a superior order of police is requisite.

When Dickens actually met these intriguing gentlemen that had to provide this new policing, he celebrated it with a piece on 'The Detective Police Party' and here he used his novelist's acuteness and sixth sense about people to give his public an insight, as when he described 'Stalker': 'Stalker is a shrewd, hard-headed Scotchman – in appearance not at all unlike an acute, thoroughly-trained schoolmaster from the Normal Establishment at Glasgow.'

After being in operation for a few years, patterns of detective duties were instituted, such as the measure of assigning two constables to keep watch on known offenders in pubs. Such men as Jonathan Whicher, a weathered and tough ex-labourer only just over the minimum height of five feet seven, worked hard to cultivate contacts and slipped easily from the police office to the sleazy world of urban crime. When it came to watching known offenders, men like him would gradually become the teachers and guides of the new men who came along. It was a school of the streets and only by walking the 'manor' and being a presence could a foothold be made.

Most regional detective departments were established after the policing revolution of the Municipal Corporations Act of 1835 and the Police Act of 1857. Amazingly, Birmingham had a detective force as early as 1839. By the 1850s the occurrence of detectives in the regions was patchy – where Middlesborough and Leeds had a few detective officers, Halifax, Wakefield and York had none. This led to journeys to the far corners of the land by 'Met men' at various times. An integral part of the social history of the detectives in the first three decades was their work beyond the capital. In fact, less than a year before the creation of the new department, Pearce had gone north to Whitby to sort out the matter of a murder in Eskdaleside, where a Mrs Robinson had been found with her throat cut, killed in the light of day. It was close to the country seat of the marquis of Normanby who had just stood down from being Home Secretary, and so it was a chance to demonstrate the prowess and sharpness of the London officers.

Pearce's trip to North Yorkshire was a successful one. A local miller called Hill had been charged and tried but there had been no bill, which meant that there was not enough evidence to support an indictment for the alleged offence. Pearce travelled in plain clothes, in order to complete the first stage of investigation all the more smoothly – listen, talk and observe things. He began to put together a narrative of likely events, and thus set a pattern for such investigations yet to come. He placed a stranger called Redhead on the scene, as he had apparently visited and been seen close to the Robinson home. He found out that Redhead had worked on the railway line about fifty miles away at Shildon, and that he was a man in financial trouble. He had been away from his place of work at the time of the murder and Pearce realised that the man could have travelled quickly between the scene of the murder and Shildon, partly on the Stockton to Darlington line. Pearce also found out that Redhead had acquired some money at just the right time to tally with the robbery on the day of the murder. He had his man. Pearce had given the new police just the fillip they needed at the right time. A top man from the Met had gone to resolve a case that local law officers (the magistrate and the constable) could not handle.

A glance at some of the detectives who typify the steady career men of the force offers an insight into the wider social context of this new work. George Clarke, for instance, was a constable in 1840, married young and then, when he became a sergeant he married again and did not live where the bachelor officers lived, number one, Palace Place. It took Clarke twenty-eight years to reach the rank of inspector. Similarly, William Palmer who joined in 1847, was an inspector after twenty-one years. Richard Tanner was a bright mind and soon rose to inspector, taking only eight years to do so. Although he died young, aged only forty-one, he was involved in some famous cases.

But of all the figures to emerge in the years between the founding of 'The Detective' and the creation of the Special Branch in 1883, Frederick Williamson and his police career illustrate the nature of the social and political context with most interest. His father was an army officer from Perthshire. Frederick was born in 1830, and as he came through the ranks he impressed and soon became a superintendent, being in command of T Division in Hammersmith. He joined the Metropolitan Police when he was just twenty-two, and transferred to the detective branch. He was a chief inspector by 1867 and Chief Constable in 1889. Known as 'Dolly' Williamson, he was energetic, athletic and ambitious for success in the force. Whicher trained him as a detective and worked with him on the notorious Constance Kent case. He was the man who took command of the CID in 1877.

The trajectory of Williamson's career illustrates many aspects of the culture of the police career of 'The Detective'. He had the extra dimension of serious scholarship, learning French at evening classes as well as normal police work; he participated in the social life of the force to a certain extent, being something of a singer. He was also a man of strength and sporting interests, particularly rowing. In other words, he had most of the traditional military qualities of the officer, but he also had wider interests and a certain strand of individuality.

His middle name Adolphus led to the nickname Dolly and he started out as a mere temporary clerk in the Ordnance Department. It is not really clear how he went up so many stages to the Detective Department, but he did, even if the right strings were pulled. Though he never became known to the public in the way that Whicher and Pearce were, he had presence and a flair for discipline and organisation as well as what we would now call 'people skills'.

In 1860 then, the department had had twenty years of life. Williamson was then a sergeant and there were still the figures from the founding phase there – some of them. There was Whicher of course, but also Tanner and Clarke. There had been one momentous event in those twenty years though – in January 1850 Commissioner Rowan retired and was replaced by Captain William Hay. Just after Rowan's retirement, the detectives were to be very much in demand when the 'Great Bullion Robbery' occurred in May 1855.

By 1860, it was firmly in the public mind that in London and some provincial towns there were now detective police. These officers had a speciality in working with the 'criminal underworld' as far as the middle class readers of *The Times* knew anything about; detectives were interesting, sometimes charismatic and in most cases puzzling creatures who had almost special powers, aspects of character separating them from ordinary mortals. The stage was set for the novelist to get to work. By that date, Dickens had already created several detectives, notably Bucket and also Mr Nadgett of *Martin Chuzzlewit*. But important events were to indicate that if there was to be a detective force, then there would have to be much more thought given to its nature and its differences from the uniformed men. There were some difficulties in the everyday professional relations of the two. In 1845 a memo was issued in response to complaints about the plain clothes men being disrespectful to uniformed officers. Mayne had to point out to Whicher and Smith that their attitudes would have to change.

This indicates that, as is totally familiar today, the detective sees a very different role for himself and consequently he assumes an identity that will follow that sense. If he has to move in two worlds and step over into the criminal world, then he has to be a very different person with special qualities. But it was a strong reprimand and it carried a threat indicating punishments for future transgressions. This was all part of a gradual shift into an acceptance of the new force. A significant detail in this development may be noticed in a memo of May 1846 in which the superintendents of each division were to select 'two intelligent constables' to be 'specially employed to observe all burglars and other felons throughout the police district and to prevent the commission of any crime by them.'

One notable feature of the detectives' lives that separates them and in some ways defines their difference is the extent to which they travelled and moved across so many locations. Consequently they found themselves having to cope with all forms of transport, gradually becoming acquainted with the wider picture of criminal fraternities and networks across the Thames basin, over the Channel and indeed within the city, where the City of London Police were developing their own detective force. The railway was only just in its initial stage of development and the police would usually travel second class. That would mean that they would have to sit with their prisoner, handcuffed to him, sitting in the open air. But this travel could mean crossing the Atlantic, as Inspector Thornton had to do in 1845. When officers had travelled north or to the Midlands to watch the Chartists, it had been at a time when most of their travel was taken by post chaise or anything else available.

But the detectives were beginning to see themselves as a special breed when Dickens met them for his series of articles. It is clear from his account of their character and their working together that they were developing a special *esprit de corps*, no doubt nurtured by their mutual reliance and their sense of shared danger, risk and enterprise. Part of this was the changing world around them and how the new police would play a part in its demands, stresses and social dissensions. Dickens was right when he said that these new men led lives of strong mental excitement. In the first thirty years of the force, such events as bombings, attempts on the Queen's life and large-scale criminal scams involving corrupt officers were to demand time, fresh lines of thought and incredible levels of energy and commitment from them.

In the major cases of the second half of the nineteenth century, there was going to be another demand on the detective branch – the area of the individual internal life, that of the psychopath and the serial killer. Little did Pearce and his colleagues in the 1840s know just how much expertise would be needed from them in terms of forensics, psychology and scene of crime analysis. They would not have used those particular words, but their instinctive habits of thought in 'good police work' would steadily be transmuted into those new sciences. In the brutal and anarchic underworld of murder, embedded in the domestic structures of the new cities those urges to homicide were to be engendered. The casebooks tell us how the new men coped with this.

4

THE FIRST DECADES:
THE MEN AND THEIR CASES

In August 1849 a worker at the London Dock customs office in Wapping was reported missing and a friend took a constable to the place where the man, Patrick O'Connor, had last been seen. It was the home of a friend of the missing man, Maria Manning. She expressed surprise that O'Connor was missing, although she had said that she had gone to his home to invite him to dinner and he had not been there. Friends worried even more and a reward of £10 for information about his whereabouts was announced. It was a mystery, and so it was work for detectives.

A Mr Flynn, who had brought in the constable, now went to Manning's home in the company of Detective Henry Barnes of Stepney, a man who was almost certainly one of Pearce's best men. There were some puzzling aspects to the Manning household – Mr Manning had not been there on both visits and Maria aroused interest to such an extent that an officer was detailed to study her behaviour at the same time that her home was under surveillance. O'Connor was a wealthy man and she had befriended him, even going to his home a few times and being very close, on good terms. A circle of friends around O'Connor were suspicious of her and they asked police to search her home. This happened, and 3, Minver Place was inspected and studied, though the details were inconclusive – there was a lot of freshly washed linen and a shovel. Even when O'Connor's private boxes were opened in case there was documentation that might lead to something, nothing was found of any consequence. But the suspicion on Maria was not lifted – she had been emotionally attached to O'Connor earlier in her life, before Manning came along. Enquiries revealed that she had gone with Manning mainly for financial reasons, as he spun a line about having money left him by his mother. The couple aroused such interest from the police now in the O'Connor case, as they had earlier been suspected of involvement in robberies from a train while Manning worked for the Great Western Railway.

What began as suspicion and progressed to surveillance and footwork ended in the finding of O'Connor's body. P.C. Barnes saw that there was wet mortar in some of the flagstones in the garden and some digging led officers to the naked body of O'Connor. He had been shot in the back of the head. But the detective work was only just beginning, and here we have the details that make this a significant case in the growth of the detective branch – both Mannings were gone and would have to be tracked down.

The first step was to issue posters with physical likenesses of the pair as line drawings. Maria had a feature that would make the search a little easier – a long scar on her face. She was French, so had she gone home? Inspector Field and Sergeant Whicher were sent to France and had help from the French police, looking into any known locations or contacts in Paris from Manning's earlier life. But more interesting is the fact that British consuls in major French cities were contacted by the detective branch. Police work was becoming international. A pursuit and search of a ship sailing out of Portsmouth led to other Mannings, not the killers, but the drama was there – two detectives boarding the SS *Victoria* after their steam yacht *Fire Queen* had gone in pursuit.

Dogged detective work, such as talking to bystanders and tradesmen, led to the information that Maria had taken a hackney cab, number 1186, and gone to London Bridge, taking a large amount of luggage with her. Sergeant Shaw did this work and he found out that she had been taken to Euston after leaving her boxes at London Bridge. Inspector Haynes opened these boxes and found letters from O'Connor and a blood-stained dress. He was on her track, and he discovered that a woman of her description had gone to Edinburgh, and the detectives now had the electric telegraph to assist them in their communication. Telegraph communication had stopped the SS *Victoria* and now it sent a message to the Edinburgh police. Mrs Manning was arrested and incriminating documents were found on her.

The search for Frederick Manning was now stepped up. As this was happening, there was massive media interest and the detective force were learning through this case, as with no other, that the drama and excitement of a detective's activities were to create crowds around Scotland Yard, expecting to see not only the murderers but the detectives as well. Evidence now showed for certain that the Mannings had planned the murder in detail. It was even ascertained that Maria had bought a new shovel the day before the killing. Manning was desperately needed now, to complete the narrative.

The hunt went on, Whicher taking part now that he had returned from France. The main focus was the West Country, and a man was actually detained and identified as Manning, totally mistakenly. But there was a Jersey connection and there he was found, detectives bursting into his room as he was in bed. On the way back for trial, he insisted that he was innocent. He said that Maria fired the gun and that she masterminded the whole affair. But it had become known that Manning had bought the lime in which the body was covered, and that he had bought a tool called a 'ripping chisel' which was used on O'Connor.

The work was done and it was now up to the court and legal process to see justice done. They were convicted and sentenced to hang and Dickens was one of the crowd (said to be around 30,000 people) on 13 November 1849 who saw the Mannings die. Afterwards he wrote to *The Times* in an argument to abolish public hangings: 'When the two miserable creatures who attracted this ghastly sight about them were turned quivering into the air, there was no more emotion … no more restraint in any of the previous obscenities, than if the name of Christ had never been heard in this world.'

The two detectives who had pursued Maria Manning to Edinburgh received £2 and 5 shillings expenses and travelled first class. The Commissioners and the Yard were just beginning to learn what real detective work entailed in terms of the budget and in the context of the kind of material support that such police work demanded.

ScotlandYard was not the only place where detectives were found how-ever. The City of London police had developed separately in their square mile and the City Fathers reorganised its staff after the 1839 Police Act, reflecting the organisation of the main police force. In 1857 one of their detectives was killed during the arrest of a desperate man, Christian Sattler. The story of how this German criminal was tracked down and apprehended tells us a great deal about the way in which detectives worked across the country, shuttling between police forces by this time. In 1857 the establish-ment of provincial forces was underway and in St Ives, Huntingdon, a Mr Ballantyne, a London stockbroker, was robbed of a bag containing valu-ables. He reported this to the local Cambridgeshire police and later enlisted the help of Charles Thain, detective of the City of London police (as his premises were in the City).

Thain and his colleague William Jarvis set to work in finding the rob-ber. He had been reported by a Cambridge pawnbroker to whom he had shown a wad of banknotes in his shop, which had made the pawnbroker suspicious. The robber, Christian Sattler, thirty-seven, was a desperate man who had spent time in Wisbech gaol and had been on the loose in East Anglia for some time. He boarded a ship to Germany after his time in Cambridge, a departure that Thain and Jarvis knew about. Thain set off in pursuit. Ballantyne and Jarvis took out a warrant but Sattler was a hard and dangerous man. He had said to his gaoler in Wisbech that he would 'shoot any man like a dog' who tried to be kind to him. If only Inspector Thain had known that. When he arrested his man in Hamburg, he set sail back home, with Sattler handcuffed, on board the SS *Caledonia*.

A short way into the journey over the Channel, on a Sunday afternoon, the prisoner complained of the pain the handcuffs caused him and asked for them to be removed. Thain resisted for some time, but appears to have relented, as the Captain testified in court: 'When I saw the prisoner he had handcuffs on – they were taken off by Thain when I went down, relieved, and put in another position. Thain wanted me present when that was done.' Later, after hearing a gun shot he, with the crew, was down in the cabin. He reported: 'Thain ... was wounded and he said he was shot. There was a gun shot wound in his right breast, and there was no medical man on board ... '

Thain had made a fundamental mistake. He was in agony for the remainder of the voyage, while the crew were all for lynching Sattler. The detective eventually died in Guy's Hospital, living just long enough to sign a statement in the presence of Sattler in the hospital ward. At the trial before Mr Baron Martin, the defence wanted to argue that Sattler had taken the gun with the intention of taking his own life, and that there was a struggle in which the detective was shot. This created a situation now familiar territory in homicide cases – the detective's struggle with the court process and the work of the defence counsel. Jarvis was firm on his insistence that his friend and colleague had been murdered. There were witnesses who said they had never heard Sattler refer to taking his own life and two witnesses were produced to quote murderous words spoken by Sattler in other contexts. Yet even then there was the possibility of a lesser charge of manslaughter. But a verdict of wilful murder was reached and Sattler hanged.

The Sattler case has several features that illustrate how and why the detectives in the mid-Victorian years were learning their profession. Thain had travelled alone with his prisoner on board ship, although he had had three German policemen with him when he boarded with Sattler. He had broken with agreed procedure and taken a risk while being alone with his man. But on the positive side, he and Jarvis had worked in collaboration with police in Wisbech, and in Cambridge, and they had searched out half a dozen witnesses who would aid the jury to see the psychopath that was Christian Sattler.

As learning experiences go, however, few events can touch the Great Bullion Robbery of 1855 in which a quarter-of-a-ton of gold was stolen from the London to Folkestone express. A criminal mastermind was at work – Edward Agar. He had an 'insider' – an ex-employee with a grudge – to supply information. Agar knew that for the safe in which the gold was kept there were two keys and two locks, and that two different employees had possession of the two keys. The chests would be weighed at Folkestone and then loaded onto the Boulogne steamer. A gang was gathered, including a man who was a train guard. What happened next in this quite unparalleled situation showed the new detective force just what ingenuity and planning could achieve in a criminal context. Agar set about making wax impressions of the two keys. He then did something that few men had ever done so methodically: he performed reconnaissance work at Folkestone and there he observed that at times there were other goods in the safe – not necessarily bullion – and that only one key would be used on these occasions. With the co-operation of his 'insider', Agar made impressions of various keys and by May in 1855 the gang were ready to act. On the night when the train was carrying gold, the insider Burgess let Agar onto the train and during the journey lead was deposited in the safe in place of the gold. Burgess and Agar escaped with the gold.

Of course, Agar was very smart. He knew that the gold had to be exchanged and re-circulated, and for this Agar had the help of the notorious 'Jim the Penman', a barrister who was also a large-scale criminal. This was James Saward, leader of what the *Annual Register* called 'The great gang of forgers'. In March 1857 he was arrested and the reports at the time took great delight in re-counting the exploits of the forgers. But in the Great Bullion Robbery, with the security arrangements seemingly perfect, there was much to be learned. The search for the culprits was indeed a challenge. Inspector Thornton and Sergeant Tanner went as far as Sweden after one villain. But as regards Agar, he was only caught as he was in gaol for another crime and had left his money with a girlfriend and another fellow thief.

The lesson was that a detective in the world of mid-Victorian Britain, a society with vastly expanding industry and communications and a huge business-fuelled economy with an empire to sustain, found himself having to match the wits of very clever, devious villains, and these villains would be 'white collar' – the enemy had more brains than brawn. The number of scandals involving fraud and embezzlement was to increase markedly in the second half of the nineteenth century and the detectives were destined to be active in that arena.

Two cases from the North West will illustrate this. The first involved the great Manchester detective Jerome Caminada; the second is one of the most notorious forgery cases ever on record – the activities of the gullible clerk Goudie in Liverpool. Both cases show very neatly what the new detectives were learning and also how the image of the detective was changing towards the end of the century. One of the main challenges to the criminal justice system and the statute law on the newer white collar crimes was to create the specialist expertise to combat the offenders. When we read Caminada's memoirs we follow the detective mind in the process of that learning curve. The son of Italian immigrants, Caminada began as a uniformed constable in Manchester in 1868 at the age of twenty-four, learning his survival skills on the streets. When he made it to detective, the detective office that was his base was in Manchester Town Hall.

By the time he joined the detective office, the *modus operandi* of adopting plain clothes and disguise was accepted. Caminada was apparently adept at this activity, being something of a 'quick change artist' and gathering a fearsome reputation for being able to slide into the criminal fraternity unobserved. He was also good with his fists and was a hard, honest officer, respected across the city by everyone who knew him. Most of his cases in the memoirs he published in his retirement concern violent robbery and domestic arguments that escalated into murder or manslaughter. But there are plenty of examples of the 'new crime' as well. His account of Elizabeth Burch represents this increasing occurrence of fraud and deception in the period which has, after all, been seen by historians as a time of economic depression.

Elizabeth Burch began as a Court dressmaker based in Sussex Place, Kensington, and worked with her two sisters. But they had financial problems and were destined for bankruptcy when, in desperation, Elizabeth hit on the idea of writing begging letters. Astoundingly, she was successful and Caminada ascribed her future career as a con-merchant to this early success. Before her arrival in Manchester, she also worked a cunning swindle in Ashford, Kent, where she profited from her ruse of pretending to be an heiress expecting £150,000 from a rich man whom she had helped one day when he collapsed in public. Burch had quickly developed the skills needed to extract cash from the gullible. When she came to Manchester the scam was linked to the Liberator Building Society as a bogus collector.

This was in 1894 and by that time Caminada was a very experienced detective. Burch had assumed a succession of false names, mostly aristocratic, after hitting on the idea of filching letter headed paper from the rich and well-connected. When Caminada finally tracked her down she was 'Lady Russell' and was indeed acting that part to perfection. He wrote in his memoirs: 'Looking at us from over the top of her gold-rimmed spectacles, she said she was connected to a titled family, was a lady of private means, and was collecting subscriptions for the people who were suffering from the recent colliery explosions in South Wales.' Caminada had to rely on tough questioning to get anything on her, and he finally arrested her on the charge of obtaining contributions by fraud. On remand, and still writing letters in the role of her assumed identity, Burch provided Caminada with a case study in deception and fraud, in terms of how the scams worked.

He learned that she would obtain documents having lists of subscribers; she would then write to them asking for money, but all done in patently legitimate and very worthy terms. Most of the names selected were women and she would write in a heavily emotional style, saying such things as 'I enclose a letter from a friend who has asked me to help the poor things. It will tell you more of their sufferings and needs than I can.' That particular letter was signed '(Lady) Marion Clarke'. Burch also had notebooks with lists of prominent Manchester people in specific areas of the city. These were people whom she called to see and gull face to face.

But now comes the most significant part of this case. An organisation called the Charity Organisation Society had been set up in 1892, four years before Burch was arrested in Manchester. In that time she had been active in all kinds of contexts in her fraudulent activities. The COS, set up by C.S. Loch, existed to monitor charitable functions and locate those who were honest and those who were not. Amazingly, Loch had known for four years that Burch was not a legitimate correspondent. Loch wrote to Caminada: 'So far as can be learned there is nothing against the character of either Miss Burch or her sisters.' The detective was astounded that the COS had not started an investigation into Burch's scams years before she arrived in Manchester.

But the Folkestone charity people thought very differently and sent Caminada plenty of information about her nefarious transactions. When Burch was in the police court for the second time, there were four witnesses collected by Caminada, including ladies from Kensington and Harrow. There was a fairly confident line of thought given by her defence – passing the buck to the aristocratic contacts who had supposedly allowed Burch to collect money for them for no profit. Poor Burch, they reasoned, duped by the powerful and lazy, and now a victim of her own good heart.

However, Caminada's hard work had paid off. Burch was sentenced to six months' hard labour in Strangeways.

The story of a huge embezzlement case at the Bank of Liverpool came to light in 1901. Thomas Peterson Goudie, a Shetlander, was a clerk in charge of the ledgers at the bank and he was foolish enough to tell some crooks at a race track that he was making forged cheques. Goudie is a significant figure in the history of the detective because his story is the first true crime narrative to be enacted on film. In the recently discovered films collected as *The Lost World of Mitchell and Kenyon*, we see two detectives escort Goudie from his lodgings in Berry Street, Bootle, to Bootle police station. Unfortunately he had not been caught by the skill or ingenuity of the Liverpool detectives, but had been shopped by his landlady, who is surely the first 'grass' to have her story told on film.

The core of the tale, and therefore where the interest lies for the challenge to the detective force, is that he was in a position of trust, inside a large company, with a responsible job, and there lay his criminal focus, his unobserved opening for crime. He was seen as a steady worker, an exemplary type for the duties of an accounts clerk. But Goudie had a weakness for gambling on horses. He gathered debts and realised that a neat way to accrue some money was to forge cheques. His £3-a-week salary would not sustain his life as a gambler. Goudie targeted Hudson, of Hudson's Soap, as he handled the firms indexed from H-K. He simply forged Hudson's name, then when the cheque reached his office after payment, he marked the journal but put no mark in the ledger under Hudson's accounts. Any checking of figures would have found him out, but he also played a part in these supervisory audits, so he kept inspection at bay whenever he could.

Goudie could not resist talking about this scam to some criminals at a race track — two men called Kelly and Stiles learned of his crime and wanted their cut, and so the blackmail began. This was followed by visits from 'heavies' to Liverpool — Goudie was a frightened man, drawing ever larger cheques to keep the threats away. When he was found out, he was asked to bring the relevant ledgers, but slipped away to try to escape into obscurity. The hunt for Goudie and his crooks were massive national news stories. His name must have been on a level with 'Capone' in terms of being public coinage in the exchange of sensation, urban myth and scandal. Then came the landlady's call at the police station and it was all up with him. Of course, detectives had been busy in the search for him and there lies the lesson. Regional detective forces relied on men like Caminada, strong and inventive individuals with local knowledge, anonymity if required, and contacts. But here was a case in which the criminal was a man with no record and had no known circle of criminal contacts. The question arose: how could detection begin when there was an offence committed by a previously 'clean' and respectable citizen? How many more Goudies would there be in this new world of massive companies and the ranks of anonymous commuters?

Meanwhile, in the world of the detective something significant had been happening. Since 1852 the private detective agency had begun to emerge. One of the men Dickens met, Inspector Field, left the Detective Branch to set up on his own. *The Illustrated Times* made Field a celebrity when it came to the major sensation of the Palmer poisoning case in Rugeley, tried at the Old Bailey in 1856. Dr William Palmer was a physician in Rugeley who had Goudie's weakness – a fondness for gambling. As his debts mounted and the pressure increased to intolerable levels, he began to see murder as the most manageable way to acquire money. His mother-in-law, one of his uncles, four of his five children, and then his wife, died with assets and insurance coming to Palmer. When his brother died after a night of heavy drinking, the insurance company would not pay up. Suspicions were aroused about Palmer when one of his friends died after treatment by the good doctor and antimony was found at the autopsy.

Obviously, such a character would attract a large amount of local hostility, and because of a new act of parliament, his trial was allowed to take place in London. The evidence from the poisoning was not conclusive and all the other evidence, though very convincing, was circumstantial. He was found guilty of murder and hanged at Stafford in June 1856. Such was the sensation and intrigue emanating from the Palmer case that *The Illustrated Times* produced a special Rugeley issue on 2 February 1856. That journal printed speculation and gossip to such an extent that it influenced the legal proceedings. Palmer was never actually charged with the murder of his mother-in-law and in fact was only tried for the murder of his friend, John Parsons Cook. But the real interest for the present purpose is how and why that journal featured Inspector Field.

There was a prominent piece headed 'Inspector Field at Rugeley' along with a biographical profile of the man, just retired from the Metropolitan Police, where he had been an Inspector in L Division and at Woolwich dockyards. He had risen to be chief of the Detective Branch and had even been active against the Chartists, so his experience did not begin and end with East End villains. The journalist behind the profile wrote, 'Fortune, fickle creature, smiled on Field, and ever since has continued to pour down upon him her bounteous gifts.'

The significant element of social history we need to note now was the nature of the life insurance business. There had been life insurance in England since the Equitable Society was formed in 1762, but it was only after the arrival of actuarial science in 1815 with Milne's mortality tables that life insurance took off. The Prudential and the Pearl arrived and specialised in working class people's policies. Palmer had taken out a policy or two, and it was the insurance firm that actually paid for Field to go down to Rugeley to do some detective work. Field discovered that Palmer had been busy insuring other, more obscure lives bearing no real link to his one, such as the curious policy taken out on a man Field found working on the land, a certain G. Bate.

Field's part in the Palmer case tells us more about the growing status and self-regard of the detective profession than about the case itself. Field had kept his title and rank on retirement, which was not considered acceptable. The Commissioner was nettled, and in the Police Orders of 7 January 1862, the following statement was made:

Restoration of pension: Mr Field, late Inspector in the Metropolitan Police, the payment of whose superannuation allowance has been stopped ... on account of his conduct in connexion with the Private Enquiry Office, has given assurance to the Secretary of State that no cause for the future shall be given for disapprobation, and that he will take steps at once to remove any impression that may exist that he acts in any connexion with the Government.

In spite of this attempt to regulate Field's behaviour in the private sphere, he did not entirely toe the line; though he was eventually still given his pension. The important point here is that the Commissioners were aware of setting precedents, and it was only too clear that any future working on crimes in which official and private detectives might be at work simultaneously was not exactly desirable.

The private detective had appeared in mid-Victorian times just as divorce became a possibility without paying for a private act of parliament. Proof was needed of marital infidelity and so there gradually arose a sleazy, unglamorous arena for private detectives to operate in. This particular variety of detection was not work for a gentleman of course; it was a case of advertising to undertake 'private watchings'. Some agencies offered to vet and study prospective spouses to be sure that the right kind of character was standing at the altar when the time came. In 1892 one journalist was still writing of the private detective as someone whose mere existence 'leaves an exceptionally offensive taste in the mouth'.

This was written by George Sala, in *Sala's Journal* for 1892. By that time, it appears that the private detective agency was almost exclusively in existence in order to shadow unfortunate victims in divorce cases. Forty years before, Harry Benson had been one of the first private detectives to create a successful company for these purposes. A later writer commenting on Benson's firm wrote: 'Between 1855 and 1860 the agency fell on very hard times indeed, due to a series of rumours put about by servants who objected to being forced to pay an exorbitant percentage of their wages for the pleasure of keeping their jobs.'

The case of Field then, seems highly exceptional and rare; the Scotland Yard men and the City of London detectives were very much in demand when it came to serious crime. Certain officers in the first two decades of 'The Detective' formed the reputation of the profession, notably Whicher, Thornton and Williamson. What most signally marked their versatility and enterprise was one of the very first examples of international terrorism and political militancy the Yard had to cope with. That it happened in Paris gave the situation the added dimension of making visible the need for the English police to liaise with the French *Sureté*.

The event was an assassination attempt on the life of Napoleon III on 14 January 1858. The intended victim. earlier known as Louis Napoleon, had led an eventful life in England before election. He had enemies, as any descendent of Napoleon would have, and what he did not do when he reached his position of power, was help to remove the Austrians from Italy. Italian émigrés in London went after him, and they were prepared to go to Paris.

What emerged was a terror ring embracing a French language teacher in London, a Chartist and a rich young rake with more money than sense. As Napoleon and his empress Eugenie arrived at the opera, surrounded by a guard of lancers, there was an explosion. Two bombs had been hurled at them and there was widespread carnage around the coach. A French *Sureté* officer came to see if the royal couple were alright and another bomb exploded. Amazingly, Napoleon and Eugenie survived, but eight people died and over a hundred were wounded, many seriously. There was work for the Scotland Yard men to do. The investigations leading backwards from the Paris events led to one Felice Orsini, who pretended to be English but was found out. As it had not been difficult to find two conspirators in Paris who were English – Chartist Thomas Allsop and the money-man Hodge – the ring of militants was soon discovered.

Of particular interest is 'Dolly' Williamson, in many ways a new breed of detective, who now found that his private French lessons paid dividends, as he was sent to arrest Dr Simon Barnard, the bomb expert. His encounter with the Frenchman was tense and dramatic to say the least. At one point the Frenchman asked to go upstairs but Williamson refused permission. Later, Barnard said to Williamson, 'You had no need to be afraid, you are English. Had you been a Frenchman I would have killed you.' Barnard had a pistol ready to use.

What emerged at the trial was something markedly modern – Mayne had assigned a police spy to watch the French and Italian refugees around London, and this had been a key element of the detective work. The spy, Sergeant Rogers, had shifted from uniform work to plain clothes to slip into the political debates at the revolutionary clubs. It was a high profile trial when Barnard stood in the Old Bailey. Whicher appeared unsuccessful in his search for the murderous Chartist Allsop. Orsini and his accomplice Pieri had been guillotined before Barnard appeared at the Bailey.

Dickens's favourite detective, Whicher, was to enter the limelight in the famous Road Hill House murder which represents a significant step forward in understanding the problems of detective work in the Victorian period and in fact since then, as the point of contention was the 'Scotland Yard Man' against the local police. The case started when on 30 June 1860, at the Kent household at Road on the Wiltshire-Somerset border, it was found that little four-year-old Francis Kent was missing from his cot. After a search, the body of the boy was found in a disused earth closet. His head was almost cut from his body and there was a deep wound near his heart. Interestingly, this gash was made after death, as it had not bled.

Sergeant Whicher was sent in response to an appeal from Sir George Lewis for 'an intelligent officer of the Metropolitan Police' to be sent to Road. When Whicher arrived, he soon realised that he was in a difficult position and he wrote to Mayne asking for help. Whicher wrote, 'I am awkwardly situated and want assistance.' Williamson was sent to him.

What was happening was that Whicher had his main suspect, the boy's big sister Constance. He had a lot to go on with regard to her possible guilt, but this was to become very little when actually in court and up against a smart lawyer from Bristol called Edlin. Whicher used his instinct and also gathered statements and opinions from a range of sources. There had been insanity on the mother's side; the girl was unhealthily interested in the life of the murderess Madeleine Smith; two medical men had told Whicher that Constance had 'homicidal tendencies'; and then one of the girl's nightdresses had been 'lost in the wash'. On the last point, any policeman would have his suspicions aroused, with thoughts of bloodstained clothes in his mind.

But Whicher was being reviled by the locals. He had been sworn in as a constable in the county of Wiltshire and he wrote to Mayne about 'the natural jealousy entertained' by the county police. He made a point of stressing that he had 'studiously endeavoured to act in concert with them as far as possible'. But Whicher's reasons for charging the girl were to prove thin and insubstantial when Edlin got to work in court. Constance Kent was released on a bond of £200 and Whicher had to face abuse and ridicule. In the course of trying to ascertain where the missing night-dress might be, Edlin pointed at the servant, accusing her of theft. He also took delight in ripping apart Whicher's character and status.

We know with hindsight that Constance Kent was guilty. She admitted her guilt in private in 1865 and then she was charged and tried. Before Mr Justice Willes she was sentenced to death but that was commuted to penal servitude for life. She was released from Millbank in 1885 and went to live in a convent. None of this would have been any comfort to poor Whicher.

The first three decades of 'The Detective' had seen the force grow from a few select men with special duties when needed, to a well established elite who worked not only with problematic murder cases in the city and in the regions but also dealt with international political crime as well. In terms of the professionalism of the officers, increasingly there were demands made on their ability to attempt dangerous and very skilful activities, including surveillance and plain clothes observation and participation in criminal networks. In the regions, by the end of the nineteenth century, the presence of detective personnel was still uneven and uncertain, with a pattern of metropolitan-local oppositions always likely, as observed in the Road Hill House murder.

What remain untouched are the trials from within the force, the temptations of power structures and quick wealth. The detectives were to be on trial and it was a trial for the whole establishment, rocking Victorian society and creating a field day for the press. Before the century was out, 'The Detective' would have to face these trials of integrity and identity from within, from the judiciary and from the government. They would also have to respond to and change in response to the arrival of the Fenians.

5

THE TRIAL OF THE
DETECTIVES : 1877

In 1860, as Scotland Yard was close to celebrating twenty years of having its 'Detective', white collar crime was nothing new to the society around it. But there had been a massive tax fraud perpetrated by James Kirkham, a clerk to the tax commissioners in Tower Hamlets; soon after his conviction the other dominoes in the line went over, including the surveyor of taxes. Kirkham's forgeries had earned him over a thousand pounds. But this offence was not a singular one; there were many others, and the worrying aspect of this was that trusted officials were involved. One corrupt official, Joseph Jay in Shoreditch, was responsible for the collection of almost £17,100 in taxes. What was arriving on the criminal scene was the spectre of nasty and planned embezzlement. The detectives now had to combat a new kind of crime, but little did they know that by 1875, their own detective officers would be part of a swindling network.

What has become known as the 'Turf Club Frauds' and also as 'The Trial of the Detectives', when the culprits were finally in court in 1877, was so unbelievably riddled with corrupt officers that it was to be instrumental in the formation of the Criminal Investigation Department. At the centre of the affair was a certain Madame de Goncourt who was so duped by the criminal minds leading the scam that she was willing to part with the huge sum of £30,000. But this network of crooks was led by two very persuasive, cunning and confident men who relished the challenge of subverting officers of the law as well as conning the wealthy citizens who fell for their clever words. Several detectives were to be on trial for their part in this, and there may well have been others who escaped investigation.

It all began when the two masterminds met. In 1874 William Kurr, often called a crafty and daring rogue, and physically robust, advertised for a writer for what appeared to be a literary enterprise. In fact it was to be a racing publication conceived to engender a 'turf club', a scam to induce people to pay for insider tips. The man who answered the advert is without doubt one of the most colourful, brainy and charismatic characters to fill the chronicles of Victorian crime. He was Harry Benson, alias Count de Montagu, and a dozen other names. Benson had just been released from prison after having duped no less a person than Alfred Rothschild out of some cash. Benson was cultured, a gifted linguist, a perfectly-groomed young man with a wealthy businessman father working in Paris. In Newgate, he had set fire to his bed and been transferred to hospital but his ruse went wrong, because he was crippled for life and had to spend another year inside.

Benson met Kurr and the partnership was destined to be lethally powerful to all who came in their sway. Kurr was daring, restless, amoral and burning for material success. Benson equalled him in that with the subtle skills of diplomacy to match. The fateful meeting of Kurr and Detective Sergeant Meiklejohn took place in 1872 and so there began a seduction of detectives who would make the scams of the two villains much more fluent in the execution. When Kurr set up his firm of Gardner &Co. in Scotland, he was already quietly confident that he and Benson could 'buy' some useful policemen.

When the two criminals expanded and started another company with targets in Europe, they had Meiklejohn in their pay, and the turning point came when they suborned a bigger fish – the young, dynamic and highly-rated Chief Detective Inspector Nathaniel Druscovich. At this time, there were around nine-hundred detectives at the Yard and Superintendent Williamson was in charge – among his senior officers were George Clarke, William Palmer and Druscovich. The latter was especially valuable because he was highly educated and multi-lingual. These men, who were to be seduced by the bribes of the leading swindlers in the scam, were very well paid – they earned between £225 and £275 a year in addition to the benefits of the rewards system still in place and of course, to the luxuries of an expense account.

Before Druscovich was to fall, Clarke had an encounter with the wily Benson, who was living as one 'Mr Yonge' at Shanklin on the Isle of Wight. The trajectory of the meeting and the corruption of Clarke provide a template for the whole cunning affair at all levels. Clarke actually had a warrant for Kurr's arrest in his pocket after good work that had found out his part in the Gardner firm. But he wrote an unsigned letter to a man called Walters and this was to be the way in to his corruption. Meiklejohn gave the letter to Benson, and Benson wrote to ask Clarke to visit him in Shanklin.

In April 1875 Clarke arrived at Benson's place. Benson, playing a clever game and acting superbly, played up his physical malformation and claimed that appearing as a witness would affect his health profoundly. He also referred to the letter that he had in his possession and it was clear that the text of that could be incriminating for Clarke. The purpose of the note was simply to set up a meeting with a crook, insisting that the meeting be kept private. It could have been construed as being 'below board'. When Benson offered Clarke £100 to make sure that he was not called as a witness, Clarke did not accept, but he had been told that other detectives were taking bribes and a foundation was laid for further overtures. Clarke did the right thing in reporting the events in Shanklin but a stream of letters from Benson gradually alarmed the officer. When he returned to see Benson, he took some cash.

The basis of the scam was that the Kurr-Benson Turf Club wrote to their victims in apparently confident and respectable terms, seemingly legitimate, but being no more than a *tip con* outfit on a grander scale. When they finally seduced Druscovich, who was desperate for money and accepted £60 from them, they became confident enough (or at least Benson was) to write to victims who would be 'bigger fish' to catch. Benson's letter to the Comtesse de Goncourt explains how the scam worked:

> Your name has been favourably mentioned to me by the Franco-English Society for Publicity, and I consequently repose in you the most esteemed confidence. What I require of you is very simple indeed. I will send you for

each race the amount which I desire you to put on the horse which must, in my opinion, win. You will have to forward the money in your name, but on my account to the bookmaker … The bookmaker will … send you the amount … This you will please remit to me and on its receipt I will send to you a commission of five per cent.

The bank Benson talked about did not exist and he had made some cheques to his own design; as the horses kept winning (of course – it was all fabricated) she kept the cheques (which were of course worthless) and she had sent £10,000 after a fairly short period. But Benson was always greedy and too daring; he approached the Comtesse for the massive sum of £30,000 and when she tried to raise the cash, her banker became suspicious.

At that point the rogues really needed their new 'bought man' Druscovich. He was sent to negotiate with Abrahams, the de Goncourt man in London, who would be on the trail of the swindlers unless Druscovich could do something about it. Basically, Druscovich bought time for Kurr to get his cheques up to Scotland and have them cashed in Clydesdale notes. He was thus doing what he and Benson did constantly in their criminal careers – change identity and travel somewhere new. But Druscovich knew he would have to play the delicate game of pretending to do something. He said, 'I must arrest someone over this job' when Kurr talked him into co-operating. It took a silver cigar-box and £200 to keep Druscovich faithful and content to carry on.

Meiklejohn was the key player though as he liaised with the other Yard men. He became greedier as the companies accrued huge assets. If we are to believe the statements made later by Benson, certain mind games had begun to be played as Meiklejohn saw just where his own position of power in the scam was. Benson recalled this very telling scene with the detective:

[Meiklejohn] 'I know exactly how much money you have changed; you have changed £13,000, and that was all profit, as you have had no expense in the advertising line.' I said, 'That may be, but of that £13,000 a great deal was our private money and secondly we have had great expense in the police line.' He said that was no business of his, what other people received, what he wanted was his own whack and that he meant to have it …

For several months the key figures, both crooks and detectives, were racing to all quarters of the British Isles. It was feared that the cat was out of the bag now that some of the men who had been cashing the bogus cheques in Scotland had been traced. This testifies to the fact that there were efficient communications between Scotland Yard and distant parts of the country. Superintendent Williamson was beginning to become suspicious but found it impossible to believe that some of his most trusted men could be bent. He wrote a memo to Meiklejohn asking for an explanation as to why he had been in Scotland, as he now knew that the detective had been there when the crooked transactions had been done. Williamson asked for some facts:

> A statement has been made to the Commissioner that from the 4th to the 6th instant you were at the Queen's Hotel, Bridge of Allan, in company with two men named Yonge and Gifford, who are wanted for committing extensive frauds. Yonge is said to have lodged with you. You are to report in explanation.

It was the beginning of the end for the corrupt detectives. When Palmer, one of the crooked officers, asked to see some letters that incriminated his colleagues, the Superintendent probably began to see that what he had suspected was true – he had some detectives on his staff who had crossed the line into criminality. An important letter from the police in Leeds was missing; strange events in Scotland were not fully explained; and now the police in Holland had an important link-man in the 'firm' in their custody and a bold attempt to have the man freed, effected by a smaller fish in the pond of crooks, had failed.

The game was almost up, and the last phase saw the rise of a future detective who would attract attention for all the right reasons – Littlechild. Druscovich had gone to Rotterdam to collect the captive, and clearly there was a plan to have him 'escape'; Williamson was suspicious and sent Littlechild after the other officers. He told Littlechild to tell absolutely no-one why he was going. He took plenty of help – a team of men in fact – and they had the knowledge of where Kurr and other gang members would be. In a moment of drama, Littlechild closed in on Kurr and the crook pulled a pistol on the young detective. The reported interchange went like this:

> 'For heaven's sake don't make a fool of yourself' cried Littlechild. 'It means murder.'
> 'I won't' said Kurr, and tamely submitted to arrest.

Kurr needed to remove anyone who knew about his connection with the de Goncourt fraud. But the one man left abroad who could get to work on that, a man called Stenning, was recognised by Littlechild and arrested. Even then Kurr did not stop scheming. There was a plan for his escape from the court cell as he awaited trial, but it failed.

Druscovich was now close to being found out. Williamson pressed him to give information about the letter from Leeds that would have added evidence to the fraudulent cheques passed in the North. He denied knowledge of it. But the fact was that now that the crook that had been paying the detectives was behind bars, the Yard men were in a precarious position and they knew it.

A Home Office investigation continued for several months which was all a matter of amassing enough definite evidence to charge Meiklejohn and Druscovich. The atmosphere in the offices and corridors must have been tense in the extreme, with most detectives who had any links at all to the suspected men being very silent, uneasy and diplomatic. It was in July 1877 that the swoop came on the turncoats. By that time, Benson and Kurr had been imprisoned and it was almost certainly due to the fact that Kurr had kept all the documentation generated by the detective he had bought. It was typical of the man that he should be so meticulous; as it was naturally a key element in his scheming to have a weapon against the police should the day arrive when his scams fell apart. That day had come and the letters and notes all helped to nail Meiklejohn and Druscovich. Benson was sentenced to penal servitude for fifteen years; Kurr, his brother and an accomplice, Bale, were given ten years.

The account of the actual arrests of the Yard men reads like a tense thriller; Clarke arrested Froggatt, an officer mainly involved in the Dutch escapade, but then was arrested himself. The other main players were taken in one by one, and the day came for the trial; it was a spectacular piece of grand opera in terms of its dramatic content as the press across the world took an interest. Here were top detectives in the dock at the Old Bailey before the great Baron Pollock, and some of them were weeping. One of the most interesting episodes was the lawyer Sir Edward Clarke's understanding of the clever and enigmatic Benson. He was defending Benson and he realised that he had to somehow change Benson's whole demeanour in order to bring out the charismatic feature of his personality that had so seduced and corrupted his charge. Prison had brought Benson down to a shell of the former dapper, suave man and a long begging letter to his father in Paris had failed to bring any material help in his plight.

Clarke saw that it was a matter of treating him like a scholar and a gentleman. He wrote in his memoir of the occasion:

> His face lit up, he rose to his feet, bowed in acknowledgment and stood with an air of deference waiting to reply … The refinement and even distinction of manner which had imposed upon Sir Thomas Dakin and Mr Alfred Rothschild again became perceptible, and while it did not influence the jury to believe his evidence, it made them think it possible that Inspector Clarke might have been deceived …

The destinies of the corrupt officers were mixed, some in eternal shame and oblivion, others emerged to try again to have some kind of second career. Clarke was the only one acquitted. Surely the grand opera came to its height when the detectives all made desperate and rhetorical pleas for mercy before the judge summed up. But they were all given two years hard labour. The only real mystery is Meiklejohn, whose ultimate fate is unknown; he worked as a private agent for some time before disappearing into obscurity. Druscovich did his stretch and then died shortly afterwards; both Clarke and Palmer became pub landlords. The most deeply criminal type in the whole ring was arguably Froggatt, as he had also been active in another fraud involving Lord Euston, so that when he walked out of the prison after his two years he was arrested for that earlier crime, and eventually died in Lambeth Workhouse.

It had been a trial at the very highest level, with premier league barristers involved in every case. Pollock was a knight in the Exchequer Division of the High Court of Justice and the counsel for the Crown included Sir John Holker the Attorney-General and Sir Hardinge Giffard the Solicitor-General. At the heart of the interplay of defence and prosecution was a markedly influential fact which Sir John Holker put very neatly when he turned to the jury:

> On the one hand, you will have to bear in mind that the evidence principally consists of statements of men whose characters will not bear investigation and who had embarked on a course of crime ... You will have to ask yourselves whether their testimony is corroborated in important details and if there is such corroboration it will be your duty to attach credence to it.

The comparatively light sentence of two years' hard labour is partly down to the nature of Kurr and Benson and partly a response to the previous good records of the detectives. To what extent their grovelling and weeping influenced the sentence is open to speculation. Druscovich appears to have convinced himself that his crimes were limited and that he perceived his transgressions were not as severe as thought. He said before going down: 'During the whole enquiry into the de Goncourt fraud, I venture to say, without fear of contradiction, I never directly or indirectly afforded them the slightest information to enable them to defeat the ends of justice.' As for Pollock, he was well aware that the sentence was lenient and pointed out that he was imposing 'a much lighter sentence than is usually awarded in cases of breach of trust of a much less important character.'

Re-reading the accounts of the main actors in the drama today, it is difficult to avoid the fascination of Benson. Here was a man made for a Hollywood movie. In his colourful life he acted dozens of roles and did so with supreme conviction. His skills were exercised on the wrong side of the law but he was so lively, appealing and entertaining that everything he did had a certain admirable boldness to it. His decline and death were in keeping with this; he was still active after release in 1887, going to America to create some bogus share certificates and later he managed to attract the daughter of a wealthy retired officer of the Indian army and was about to extract the huge sum of £7,000 from her father's assets when he was found out. Even then he wriggled out of it and fled once more across the Atlantic.

His last days are almost tragic, as they reflect the lowly and intolerable condition of a man with flair and personal magnetism. He was locked away in Tombs gaol, New York, and while walking in a line of inmates high above a wing one day, he ran and plunged to his death over a railing.

The Trial of the Detectives lasted twenty-six days; one of the central issues was that conspiracy was a common law offence, and although this was punishable by hard labour it still presented a problem to the judiciary. This specific example of duplicity and corruption within the very ranks of those who were trusted to protect the public and combat criminals, was something that tested the machinery of law, including statutes and precedents, to the extreme. But one thing the whole unpleasant business did achieve was the creation of the CID. A Home Office Departmental Commission had been investigating the structure and functioning of the detective force from a point just before the trial and the principal members of the enquiry met four days before the trial ended. A barrister called Howard Vincent was to take control of the new department, with a rank of Assistant Commissioner. He was a man who had been influenced by continental methods and had no qualms about using *agents provocateurs*. He brought out a Police Code (clearly intended in part to show the public that the 'Turf Fraud' kind of corruption was going to be a thing of the past) and this was to be constantly updated. The new man also increased the salaries of detectives and reinvented the *Police Gazette*, to some extent influenced by Henry Fielding over a century before. The ideology of the *Sureté* is evident everywhere in the man who conceived of the CID.

Vincent's fondness for what would now be called 'entrapment' was made apparent in the case of a chemist called Titley who was involved in illegal abortion activities. A 'plant' who was in fact the wife of a police officer posed as a customer for Titley; he sold her the requisite drugs and was entrapped and charged. This was a very 'un-English' move. There was such an outcry that the Home Secretary had to go through the motions of indicting the officers in plain clothes, but that fizzled out.

Vincent had shown these predilections before coming to power, having written a report on the French detective system – the brainchild of the great Vidocq of the previous generation. The first stage in an inevitable change of identity was taking place under Vincent's leadership. This new, more cosmopolitan and less restrained form of detective work was to be met with criticism and opposition, and was slated by one writer as 'an entire failure in every respect'. The signs of the times were wholly apparent after the Fenian bombing at Clerkenwell in 1867, ten years before the Trial of the Detectives, when criticisms had been levelled at Mayne who by then had done thirty-eight years of service. The Earl of Derby wrote:

> It is really lamentable that the peace of the Metropolis, and its immunity from wilful destruction, should depend on a body of police who, as detectives, are manifestly incompetent; and under a chief who, whatever may be his other merits, has not the energy nor apparently the skill to find out and employ men fitted for peculiar duties.

The Clerkenwell bombing had killed 12 people and injured another 120. A small detail that today would command the attention of every passing constable, enabled the Fenians to carry out that mass killing – a barrel left against the wall of the House of Correction. The disaster was not so much the result of poor detective work – it was poor everyday policing of the streets.

But the new professionalism of the CID was clearly apparent in the structure and the staff: the new outfit, under solicitor J.E. Davis for administration and Vincent for general control, had sixty divisional detective patrols and twenty special patrols. There was a regulating body of sergeants – 159 in number. A shift system would operate and there would be tighter supervision down the ranks, with fifteen Detective Inspectors at the top. A division between the Yard and the CID men was established and that tradition, whereby the CID men stayed with the CID, remained in place until Sir Robert Mark's regime changed things in the 1970s.

There had been a significant step forward in terms of the more political arm of detective work back in 1867 when an army man, Lt.Col. W.H.A Fielding, started a secret service operation. It was clear from that point that there were going to be increasing specialisms within the broader range of detective work. The whole profession was becoming demanding in different ways, and this is exemplified by the footnote to police history that relates to Sergeant Lear from Shropshire, a man who had to track his suspect for a hundred miles, travelling on foot, in 1871.

The 'peculiar duties' referred to by the Earl of Derby in his criticisms were to be far more onerous, demanding and radically different from past procedures than anyone realised, with the coming of the phenomenon of the serial killers Jack the Ripper and Charles Peace. Both cases illustrate the nature of this more accelerated, mobile and highly-populated world that they had to police. The police corruption had taught the top brass about internal disintegration and the challenge from inside the Yard's own structures: now in Whitechapel and the regions there was a new threat to their competence and organisation. What was about to be tested, more than anything else in the responsibilities and structures of the detective force, was the efficiency of their work at two important levels: first in their communication methods across city and provinces; and second, in their supervision and monitoring of the population in those city areas in which dissidents, radicals and alienated individuals resided.

'Peculiar duties' were soon to become far more specialised than Derby ever dreamed or Vincent himself could have imagined, though his knowledge of Paris and the methods of the police in the Napoleonic period would be an asset.

6

HUNTING JACK THE RIPPER
AND CHARLIE PEACE

Sunday 13 November 1887 became known as 'Bloody Sunday' as it involved a particularly nasty confrontation between the police and a motley assortment of rebels and radicals. It was an event that, with hindsight, can now be seen as profoundly informative about the upheavals of that period. The Chief Commissioner of the Metropolitan Police at the time was Sir Charles Warren, and he was to step down in 1888 just as the Ripper enquiries were in progress. The few years around the horrendous public disorder and the unbelievably brutal killings in Whitechapel were also years in which Warren had problems within his own corridors of power.

All these factors made the Jack the Ripper murders fascinating for press and public alike for many years, because the arrival of the psychopathic sexually manic killer was to push the resources of the detective officers to the limits before the spate of murders stopped in November 1888. The five murders definitely attributed to Jack happened within the months August to November 1888, although October (strangely the month with extensive fog around the streets) was homicide-free in this context. For the history of detectives and detection, the principal interest is in how the fairly new CID dealt with the case and how the various categories of officers worked together.

At the heart of the murder investigation is the nature of Whitechapel itself. As many 'Ripperologists' have pointed out, although the repressive measures against working class people had been harsh, the area at the time was far from antipathetic to the police. Warren had concentrated on the discipline and organisation of the uniformed police and quite sensibly responded to the 'war' in the streets – Fenian bombs, violent radicals and rioters on the rampage. But now along came the serial killer and what was to be done? The Ripper killings provide us with a chronicle of the detectives at work against a criminal mind, sick to the core, that they did not have any means of understanding. In practical terms, they had no fingerprinting – that was to come much later. What they did have was common sense, pragmatic sense and a grasp of police procedure.

Ironically, there was something in the Zeitgeist that sensed that this new alienated and homicidal criminal with a motive would be easily categorised. Not long before the murder of Mary Ann Nichols in Buck's Row, Whitechapel in August 1888, R.L. Stevenson had published *The Strange Case of Dr Jekyll and Mr Hyde* (1886) and the first Sherlock Holmes story *A Study in Scarlet* appeared in *Beeton's Christmas Annual* for 1887. A cursory survey of the murder cases across the country in the ten or fifteen years around 1880 shows the reasonably logical trend that murders were still mostly committed in domestic circumstances by killers known by the victim – but the changes in community identity were also beginning to be reflected in the murder cases.

Looking back at that period, it can be seen that it was a period of accelerated change in terms of the new commuter class and of what the sociologist Durkheim has called 'anomie'. Traditional cohesion in working class communities steadily disintegrated, particularly in London and other major cities, and along with that came a more common occurrence of anomie – the sense of identity and communal purpose being taken away, meanings and patterns of known justifications for actions being blurred. The years *c.*1870–90 were years in which the city became a metaphor for this anomie and loss of community – a location for disenchantment, loneliness and sociopathic feeling. Gothic fiction such as Stevenson's explored the nature of transgression and disorder within the self, the closeness of barbarity to what Victorians were wont to dwell on as desirable 'civilisation'. After all, in 1857, the British Empire exercised its civilising qualities by firing cannons through the bodies of Indian mutineers and the British police in 1880 were handy with their truncheons, for which a special new pocket had been introduced in 1887.

Here was the CID then, along with the detectives of Scotland Yard and of the City force, in most senses maintaining the same ideology of policing as their uniformed colleagues: still military but now with detective methods that in many ways paralleled the methods of military espionage as first practised against political radicals and later against the enemy in the outposts of empire. Their knowledge at the time that the Ripper appeared was practical, but also locked into the crimes emanating from the community, rather than from forces alienated from it. Worse still, the Ripper killings were on prostitutes, the workers of what was then seen as a sad but necessary industry for those women who had fallen and were still falling.

The murder committed just before the first definite Ripper killing was that of Emma Smith, who had been set upon, raped, and killed by a gang of drunks. That kind of crime, though it involved the use of a blade in her vagina, was an extension of the drunken brutality common at the time. Yet when Nichols was killed, the sheer level of destruction to flesh and organs of the victim was of a previously unknown nature. A clear way to understand the process of the work done by a detective when faced with such a case is to look at Inspector Frederick Abberline of Scotland Yard who stepped in as matters intensified, to help the team under Inspector Reid of H Division and Joseph Helson of J Division. Abberline was a seasoned policeman who knew the East End very well indeed: for most of his twenty-five years in the police he had worked in Whitechapel; he was local Inspector for H Division in the years 1878–1887; and he knew the gangs and fences very well. Not long before the Nichols murder he had been assigned to work at Scotland Yard because the top men in the CID wanted him there: both Williamson and Munro backed that move, and Munro was the Assistant Commissioner of the CID. So Abberline had just left his 'patch' with a sense of near retirement in his head, when he was called back, as the best man to sort out the Whitechapel monstrosities.

For Sir Charles Warren, it must have been some kind of relief to have a focus for his energy at this time: he was in conflict with the CID which cannot have helped the direction of the Ripper enquiries at the highest level where the important decisions were made. He was the army man responsible for keeping the police generally at full levels of efficiency and against him was the CID Assistant Commissioner, James Monro. It seems that Monro – with political responsibilities and a full awareness of the objectives of the CID in a more international sphere – believed in autonomy from the 'army' of the police as Warren saw it. Some commentators have seen this as a contributing factor to the failure of the police in dealing with the Ripper killings, but Philip Sugden has satisfactorily settled that view as unfounded. Sugden insists that Warren was not 'a military despot' and that he had been much maligned. Arguably, the real significance of this row at the very moment that the Ripper was raging his terror in the streets is that it highlights the lack of any real understanding that the leading detectives had of 'serial killing' then.

Abberline's mind at work is seen very clearly in his report written just ten days after the third murder of Annie Chapman on 8 September (she counts as the third death if we include Martha Tabram, a likely candidate for being a Ripper victim). Abberline and his team worked hard but had no definite results. He wrote his report a few days after Chief Inspector Donald Swanson took over central control of the Ripper investigations, and must have been aware that he should be particularly methodical. Swanson was to write extensive notes on the whole course of the Ripper years.

Abberline began by describing the finding of Nichols' body by two car men at 3.40 a.m. on 31 August. Astounding by today's standards, he notes that 'they did not notice any blood and passed on'. Later, when constables and doctors arrived on the scene, the horrible extent of the injuries was observed. Inspector Spratling arrived later and he took it upon himself to study the extent of the wounds on the corpse before it was taken to the mortuary. He was smart enough to see that the wounds on the stomach were made before those to the throat. But the most notable piece of detective work that Abberline accounts for is the tracing of the woman's identity through a mark on her underclothes indicating Lambeth Workhouse. The detective's summary of her life and descent is a remarkable insight into the impartiality and perfunctory attitudes such a man had to have: ' ... she had been separated about nine years through her drunken and immoral

habits and that for several years she had from time to time been an inmate
of various workhouses …'

What is witnessed in the reading of Abberline's thoughts and reflections
is a confrontation between the utilitarian officer of the law who knows
the community he works in, and the dark exterior forces of alienation.
The weak and vulnerable of that community had been selected as keenly
and efficiently as a stray calf by a lioness. Abberline tried to understand the
motive – that was his accustomed line of thought. For instance, three men
were working only thirty yards away at a slaughterhouse and they would
have to be top of the list for questioning. Abberline notes: 'No grounds
appeared to exist to suspect them of the murders.'

The thoroughness of the investigation is then impressive, including a persistent chase for soldiers seen on the fateful night, leading to an identity
parade and a most untrustworthy witness. Abberline then falls back on the
last resort: such a killer, with an apparent motive no more complex than a
sadistic bloody frenzy, must be insane, and the detective had a thought: 'I
beg to add that the man Isenschmid who was detained at Holloway on 12th
instant and handed over to the parochial authorities as a lunatic, is identical with the man seen in the Prince Albert at 7 a.m. on the morning of
the murder.'

What then began to develop after the failure to find a suspect and make
an arrest was a press feeding-frenzy in the midst of a moral panic which
had already seen the formation of a vigilante group, a situation that we are
familiar with today. But if we now return to the nature of the Whitechapel
area and its population, it is to find interesting elements and trends that
surprisingly show a populace not at all antagonistic to the police, even if
the press men were. Several historians have pointed out that although the
streets around Whitechapel Road and Commercial Road were a laby-
rinth that could still be legitimately called a 'rookery' where criminals and
fugitives could escape scrutiny, it was changing for the better at that time,
partly because of a swathe of new immigrants. Jewish émigrés from Eastern
Europe were arriving: there had been vicious pogroms of Jews by the forces
of the Tsar in 1881–2 and the builder of German unity, Otto von Bismarck
had evicted the Poles from Prussia in 1886. These were destined to be

people who wanted to work hard, save and prosper. They had a business instinct, and Victorian Britain, with its ethos of self-help, was tailor-made for success if a communal spirit was mixed with a personal application to work. Such people would certainly not welcome prostitutes in their midst. Around 1850, Henry Mayhew had listed fifty markets in Whitechapel; he noted the contrast between the honest working man and the fallen; types who descend like Nichols to the common lodging houses: 'I heard from several parties of the surprise and even fear with which a decent mechanic – more especially if he were accompanied by his wife – regarded one of these foul dens.'

Even by the 1860s, Mayhew was monitoring the differences between what he called 'street Jew-boy' and the 'decent Jew' who knew their religion. It seems to be the case that the newer Jewish immigrants who were infiltrating and even 'gentrifying' parts of Whitechapel existed in opposition to the more well-known areas where radicals and subversives tended to lodge. This social context explains the muddle with reference to the enigmatic scrawl written on the doorway entrance jamb over the place where Eddowes was attacked on 30 September: 'The juwes are the men that Will not be Blamed for nothing.' The Jewish population in the area was established long before the recent pogroms, however. Sephardic Jews had been in that part of London since the mid-sixteenth century and there had been a synagogue in Aldgate since 1752.

The working people of the area appear to have been well aware that the beat system was a comfort to them in the dark streets, and that there had been officers soon on the scene after the Nichols murder; but they also acted as they had always done – taking upon themselves a role of self-help and self-regulation. They became vigilantes. This was all very well, but it contributed to the press criticisms and satires. If we turn to the media and the detectives in the Ripper period we see another major feature of the history of Scotland Yard (and of the City of London detective branch) that figured prominently then and has been problematic ever since: the relation between the media and the police detective.

Much of the antagonism and misunderstanding between the fourth estate and the detective branch was based on the fact that at the very centre of the Metropolitan Police ethos was a belief that there should be a tight-lipped approach to the inevitable press curiosity. Journals such as *Police News* were always eager to depict scenes from criminal and penal life with a sense of drama; even *Punch* and *Illustrated London News* were generally more interested in stereotypes than truth. But the phenomenon of the detective in such an affair as the Ripper's reign of terror was destined to be severely critical, as it was the cause of moral panic and led to a desire to create the paranoia that always accompanies such crime.

Of course, the intervention of the press in police investigation is not all negative; the CID had however insisted that no information be imparted to newsmen, and so received very little publicity of the beneficial kind. The tendency was for the papers either to create a totally fabricated occasion for fear, or to search for possible causes on their own rather than await police information. A template example of this was in the panic over the garrotting menace of 1862-3. At that time a new variation on vicious robbery had developed, with a gang of three men working as a team to accost, garrotte and rob victims in the street. The press placed the blame for this terrifying phenomenon on the 'ticket of leave men' – the convicts who had gained early release on a system similar to licensing in the contemporary criminal justice system. The papers and periodicals were flooded with images of garrotting and of citizens taking self-protection precautions such as carrying a sword-umbrella or walking at night with hired guards.

Howard Vincent of the CID stipulated the one acceptable reason for telling newsmen anything about a case:

> The press is a power to detect crime which we must not omit to take into account … and when publicity is desirable their help is invaluable. Indeed, if the identity of a culprit is clear, and the importance of a case is sufficient, the question of his capture is reduced to a mere question of time and money.

But if there is no lead about a killer and the investigation is embedded in theory and speculation, the press must be kept at arm's length.

On that point Vincent wrote, 'Police must not on any account give any information whatever to gentlemen connected with the press.'

In the Ripper year the story of 'Leather Apron' illustrates very clearly the consequences of press elaboration and embellishment of narratives in order to have some copy when the information from official sources is not forthcoming. If ever an instance was needed to show the nature of a moral panic it was the Jack Pizer story. Pizer was a pimp who used and threatened prostitutes and his name came up during the Nichols investigation. Somehow, possibly from a careless statement by a policeman or even from an overhead conversation, the papers heard about Pizer, known as 'Leather Apron'. The detectives wanted to be sure that Pizer was not the Ripper, as he was clearly violent against women and at work in the Whitechapel area from time to time. In the popular press, suddenly Leather Apron was a Ripper suspect: 'The strange character who prowls about Whitechapel after midnight – Universal fear among the women – slippered feet and a sharp leather-knife,' so printed *The Star*.

Of course, the main contribution of the press as far as it affected the detectives' work, was to heighten the mystification of what a detective actually was and how he conducted his work in such terrifying places as the courts and alleys of the East End. The same public that eagerly awaited the latest Sherlock Holmes story read *The Illustrated Police News* on Saturday and there they saw graphic accounts of the gothic narrative of the killer stalking by night, amoral and ruthless. This periodical was not an official police publication, though the title makes it seem that way. After the Mary Kelly murder on 9 November, for instance, this paper reported the story using phrases such as 'lured to the slaughter' and 'a mysterious man with a black bag.' After the Nichols murder, the journal depicted the story in pictures, in addition to the detailed account of the mutilations expected by its readers. Interestingly, the detective involved, Inspector Helston, is sketched in a small portrait in a gallery along with P.C. Neil, the coroner and Dr Llewellyn. But as time went on, and as the silent participation of the detectives on the case became more and more intriguing, the detectives began to figure more in the mystery of the tale. This is illustrated in a piece from a later issue headed, 'scenes and incidents of the mystery of the East End' in which a woman's face is shown with the caption 'a disguised detective ready for the Whitechapel monster' and then in a dark court a man is 'shadowed by a detective disguised as a female.'

The same paper gave open criticism of the police and notably the detective branch in its 24 November issue, showing 'Scotland Yard Asleep' during the 'London Murder Scare' and there we see a detective and two uniformed men snoozing while a murder takes place 'opposite a policeman's bedroom window.' This referred to the murder of Mary Kelly, the last killing, on 9 November; the police could not have imagined a worse press image: a police constable lived on Mitre Square where Kelly was murdered.

By the end of the ordeal, dozens of detectives were working shifts of around fourteen hours a day and no solid progress had been made. Warren made a desperate statement on 4 October that is astounding in its pragmatic bafflement: 'I am quite prepared to take the responsibility of adopting the most drastic or arbitrary measures that the Secretary of State can name which would further the securing of the murderer, however illegal they may be.'

If nothing else, what with the Ripper's reign of terror and its mediation in the popular press running alongside the incredible success of Sherlock Holmes, the mystique and appeal of the detective in the popular imagination only intensified. Detectives were parodied in literary journals and caricatured along with the uniformed men. But the writers did their part to heighten the interest. To take merely a few examples from the Ripper period: Dick Donovan in *The Strand* magazine, a detective superhero against arch-villains; Robert Barr, who invented Valmont the French detective; and most celebrated of all, Wilkie Collins and his novel *The Moonstone* (1868). Of course, most fictional detectives were private investigators (like Holmes) and we must not overlook the importance of Inspector Lestrade in the Holmes stories. In response to Lestrade's delivery of his theory in *The Norwood Builder*, Holmes says to the Yard man: 'It strikes me, my good Lestrade, as being just a trifle too obvious,' said Holmes. 'You do not add imagination to your other great qualities; but if you could for one moment put yourself in the place of this young man, would you choose the very night after the will had been made to commit your crime?'

By the last decade of the nineteenth century, writers and journalists appeared to want to denigrate the detective force and to celebrate the amateur, but at this point it is worth recalling that there had been notable victories by the official detectives, and plenty of real-life action to rival the fictional sleuths, as in the story of Charles Peace, from a decade before the Ripper appeared. Peace was so famous that in a Holmes story, Conan Doyle made reference to Peace – a violinist like the Baker Street genius – as a man respected and complimented for his musical skill.

In 1884, there was a proposal to appoint a Director of Public Prosecutions to take some of the work from the belaboured Treasury Solicitor's Office and to back the police investigations into the proliferation of receivers of stolen goods across the country. This important step forward in establishing support mechanisms for detective work was, ironically, the outcome of the Charles Peace case. Peace, when finally captured, gave the police a list of such criminals across the land and the centre of such illegal commerce – London – was investigated as a first step. This was arguably the one beneficial outcome of the staggeringly eventful life of an arch-villain whose name permeated popular culture almost as much as the Ripper, but who is perhaps most productively compared with the likes of Jack Sheppard and Dick Turpin in the previous century.

Peace was born in Manchester in 1832. His father was an animal trainer. The events of his life are a mix of recorded fact and sheer urban myth, the product of eager journalists; but the fact remains that, as a factor in the history of the detective, his story is significant. This is mainly because the hunt for the man (who had multiple identities) meant that detectives would have to move from north to south and from one local piece of police liaison to another. In addition, his crimes entailed a more refined and streamlined version of detection of identity than was normal.

He suffered an accident in a mill when he was young, and so Peace had an artificial part made for his arm. He was distinctive in many other ways too, so in theory would have been very easy to spot when a constable was in pursuit. But the story does not end there: he was a master of disguise and was skilled in the art of gurning – he could manipulate his jaw to change the appearance of his face. Peace's appearance was therefore most striking, as W. Teignmouth Shore described in the volume on Peace in the *Notable British Trials* series, where he quoted a police description:

> He is thin and slightly built, from fifty-five to sixty years of age, but appears much older; five feet four inches high, grey (nearly white) hair, beard and whiskers … He lacks one or more fingers on the left hand, walks with his legs rather wide apart, speaks somewhat peculiarly as though his tongue was too large for his mouth, and is a great boaster.

One would expect such a singular character to be observed and apprehended very easily when the police wanted him for enquiries. But he was always hard to find, shifting from one identity and lifestyle to another. He had exceptional artistic skills, including being a very talented violinist; he lived as a picture framer and carver; and he also managed to carry on his burglary while engaged in these occupations part time. After being released from Chatham gaol in 1872, however, his criminal career was to move from burglary and larceny to murder. Between 1872 and 1875 his career is obscured by slender details and much myth-making. He was already a popular figure in the Yorkshire press by the time he committed his first murder: the shooting of P.C. Cock in Manchester in 1876. Two brothers were arrested for that murder, at Whalley Grange, and one was given the death sentence, though it was commuted.

With his first killing done, he moved to Sheffield and there he began to harass the wife of a Mr Dyson who lived a few doors down from Peace and his family in Banner Cross. Mrs Dyson made the mistake of encouraging Peace's romantic interest in her and the Dysons tried to evade Peace by moving house. Peace tended to appear and confront the woman, obviously engaging in a reign of fear. At one time he came to her and said, 'I'm here to annoy you, and I'll annoy you wherever you go.' Peace persisted in this shadowing of his victim, and one night, as Mrs Dyson came outside her house to the water closet, there was Peace. When she screamed, Mr Dyson ran out, and Peace shot him twice.

It is after that second murder that Peace's career started to have an effect on the detective branch; he moved to London and stepped into a new identity: John Ward, a gentleman of leisure, and burglar by night. His distinctive mode of work was to travel to the designated venue for the theft in his pony trap, and he always had his tools in his violin case. But he very nearly committed murder number three in Blackheath when he shot another police officer. But he was caught and in custody simply as 'John Ward' until he was too bold and took the risk of writing to a colleague, so making his John Ward ruse open to police knowledge when they talked to the man in receipt of the letter. Peace was also 'grassed' by his woman friend, Thompson.

It might have been the end of Peace's dramatic life: the police now knew that he was wanted in Sheffield and he would have to be taken north to Leeds for trial. But, according to one account, as they neared Darnall on the train north he said to one of his guards 'That's Darnall, where I used to live. Open the window and let's have a breath of fresh air.' One of the warders did so, and Peace leapt through the opening. One man grabbed Peace's leg and there was a struggle. The murderer kicked so hard that he lacerated the hand of the guard and the boot came off. Peace was free, rolling off the train at high speed. When the guards ran back for him, the criminal was dazed and seriously hurt. He was recaptured and eventually stood trial at Leeds assizes.

He was found guilty of murder on 4 February 1879 and sentenced to death. His story was the next big sensation to fill the papers after the battle of Rorke's Drift in the Zulu War. The 'King of the Burglars' as some media called him, confessed to the Manchester killing and the Habron brothers were cleared.

As an early writer on Peace wrote: 'Charles Peace was a man of considerable gifts: of that there can be no doubt. As a detective he might have been the greatest ever known in England. As an actor he should have succeeded admirably.' This may be an overstatement, but his case does give us an insight into the work of detectives at that time – just at the same time as the racecourse fraud, in fact. One of the most interesting details is in the work of Detective Phillips in London after the arrest of 'John Ward'. The detective work conducted during the saga of Peace's criminal life emerges most clearly in the trial of Hannah Peace on 14 January 1879.

Hannah was on trial for receiving, and Inspector Henry Phillips investigated her case after Peace's arrest. The significance of the case is clear in Phillips's account of his enquiries:

> From enquiries I made I went down to Darnall, which is about 5 miles from Sheffield, on 5 November. The house I went to was occupied by William Bolsover, his wife, sister, the prisoner, and Willie Ward. I sat down and had some conversation with them and told them I had come from Peckham. I turned and saw a clock on the drawers, which I knew from a description to belong to a Miss Dodson of Blackheath. Inspector Twybell came in, and I told the prisoner and Bolsover that the clock was stolen property and that I should take charge of it …

Phillips found a large box with a massive amount of property in it, stolen during Peace's burglary regime at Blackheath. What had happened is important to our understanding of the long process of education required of the detectives at the CID (Phillips was attached to the CID). By the 1870s there was clearly a reasonable level of communication between the London men and the regions, and after the work on ascertaining the identity of 'John Ward' the system worked: leads were successfully followed to Sheffield, and from that eventually the Treasury were involved, as they had prosecuted Hannah at this trial.

What began to emerge in the ranks of the detective force in the 1870s was the fuller recognition of the tendency of criminals to make a study of police methods, and also to spend more time conceiving of new varieties of crime. But there was always a difference in perception in the criminal classes of the 'Smoke' in terms of how they saw the 'Met' and how they saw other, provincial forces. One ex-police officer explains in his memoirs that, in referring to London villains:

'There is nothing special about them ... On being questioned, the answers they gave were just as expected and they gave me the impression that they regarded themselves as being too clever to be caught by country policemen.'

The more sophisticated and savvy men of the later decades of the nineteenth century had become an integral part of the criminal underworld, working their way into the microcosm infested by the 'fences' and the specialists in particular burglaries or scams. They must have heard crooks saying Bart Simpson's words a thousand times: 'I didn't do it, nobody saw me do it, you can't prove anything.' But it is a tendency in the growth of plain clothes police work to meet brains equal to their own, as other more general forces start to work on the nature of crime in each generation. Cases such as those of Charles Peace and Jack the Ripper were so large and constantly generating new consequences to every move made by detectives in the 'chase', that those narratives were certain to change the nature of the detective force – and from the top.

By 1878 there was a recognised need for a new police headquarters and the commissioner at that time, Sir Edmund Henderson, had his eyes on a site very close to New Scotland Yard. Something fresh was needed, something of larger scale. The thinking was that if the CID was to be streamlined and the whole police structure redesigned, then a new base was required. Two years later there was more pressure to accomplish this task, and eventually £186,000 was paid for the site. Norman Shaw was commissioned to design a new building and the CID wanted forty offices for themselves in the new place. When the new home for the police HQ finally appeared in 1890 there were several criticisms but just before Christmas that year the Commissioner and his staff moved into their new rooms and another phase in the history of the Yard had begun.

This came after one of the most significant developments in the history of detectives in England – the establishment of the Special Branch. We must now retrace our steps and consider the impact of Fenianism and the nature of what Sir Robert Peel had called 'political police'.

7

SPECIAL BRANCH: SECTION D - 1888

On 15 March 1883 as Parliament debated issues around naval reserves, and the Home Secretary was in the Commons enjoying a meal, there was an explosion. Someone had put a bomb near the Charles Street government offices. With an attack so close to the heart of the State and Empire, it was time for urgent action. Five days later, because the American-based Fenians had almost certainly been responsible, an Irish Bureau was established in Scotland Yard.

Adolphus 'Dolly' Williamson took charge and his brief was to gather twelve top detectives and work with the intelligence department headed by Robert Anderson. The new office was in Great Scotland Yard, close to the Rising Sun public house. It did not take long for this new group to be called the Special Irish Branch. It was a development of the tendency to assemble teams of men with special expertise to tackle specific threats or new crimes, such as the garrotting panic of 1862 in which police had to rethink attitudes to street crime and to violent crime in general.

But this was different. It was not realised at the time but what happened was the beginning of a split in the Yard that would become significant in the history of the detective in England: detectives would now work in liaison with the military intelligence people, the Home Office and the Foreign Office in pragmatic response to events on the world stage rather than merely domestic matters. That fact was to be the cause of rifts, jealousies and resentments in the ranks, and it also opened up the potential for powerful and ambitious individuals to make a name for themselves in new areas of detective work. Henceforth, some detective officers found themselves acting in quasi-espionage situations and as time went on, in real espionage.

The ultimate cause of this had been the activities of the Fenians. After the general historical process of the absentee landlords and then the great famine in Ireland, a large number of Irishmen crossed the Atlantic to fight in the American Civil War of 1861–5. There was a feeling that a war between Britain and the United States was possible and they hoped to fight on the American side. New York, with its thriving Irish-American community, provided the natural base for operations. Fenianism was a political and nationalist ethos, republican in aims and violent in its methods. One of the most important leaders, O'Donovan Rossa, was arrested in 1865 and by the next year the government began to see that bombing campaigns in London were going to be a constant threat.

A bill to suspend Habeas Corpus was passed in February 1866 and the Lord Lieutenant was given special powers of arrest. It was controversial in the extreme: John Bright criticised it as 'a blot upon the reign of the Queen'. The most notable result of this was that Americans in Ireland, who had been building alliances with republicans, went home. The focus of activities was going to be across the ocean and that would have important consequences for the new detectives. The Habeas Corpus principle was one of preventing arrests on suspicion and also of making it illegal for a person to languish in gaol for indefinite periods. It also dictates that every person has a right to trial by jury. In other words, the suspension was an act familiar to Britons today – it was a response to terrorism.

There was a history of Fenian bombing and the Special Irish Branch was well briefed on that. Williamson had been active during the first real campaigns of 1867. That had been a period of desperation and extremism on the part of the Fenians. In 1866 a force of Fenians had tried to invade Canada after capturing Fort Erie. In 1867 they had attempted to attack Chester Castle and in 1867 they at last had a terrible impact on English life. Although a rising led by James Stephens had failed in Ireland, the war was carried into England. On 8 September 1867 a police officer, Sergeant Brett, was murdered in Manchester while guarding two Fenian prisoners, Kelly and Deasy. The killers were executed, thus providing the Fenian movement with martyrs who became known as 'The Manchester Martyrs'.

On 13 December that year came the Clerkenwell explosion. Twelve people died and sixty yards of prison wall were ruined. Over a hundred people were wounded. If nothing else, these events had the effect of making English people aware of the issues in Irish society. Between these first major terrorist activities and the new scares of the 1880s, Gladstone fought for reform with regard to the Irish questions of Home Rule and changes in the established Church. But even during the new bombing campaign in the 1880s, the Home Rule bill was defeated.

Detective work was moving into the political arena. It was only logical that leaders would come along who would be very different from the military men and the 'through the ranks' personalities such as Williamson. In other words, there was a need for a spy network which would operate aside from the detectives, but obviously needing their help on occasion. The 'spymaster' who emerged was a strong personality with an eccentric streak in him – Edward Jenkinson, a man who loved working in disguise and who had a penchant for cloak and dagger adventure. By 1884 James Monro was heading the CID, following Littlechild, and he was becoming increasingly aware that Jenkinson was going to be difficult. The spymaster insisted on working in his own way, with information kept back from the CID. He saw himself and his network as being separate from detectives and this was a growing rift as the years went on.

Jenkinson had emerged as a prominent figure in this respect after being Under-Secretary for Police and Crime at Dublin Castle after the Phoenix Park murders of 1882, in which the Chief Secretary for Ireland Lord Frederick Cavendish and Thomas Burke, his secretary, had been stabbed to death in that Dublin park. In London, in his new position of power, he began to develop a network of double-agents, 'spooks' and real agents wherever he thought there was a possibility of a bomber-group being formed. This meant planting agents in such places as Mexico, Paris and New York. Later, it also meant that he would need links with Russia, as by 1885 there was a strong possibility that the old machinations of the

'Great Game' of espionage based on the Russo–British rivalry for control of the Levant and of India, would be renewed.

But after a long series of bomb-scares, myths and fabrications which cost a great deal of money, Jenkinson was sacked. Arguably, the only real achievement of his reign was to show that detectives were perhaps the best types of personnel to work on 'Royal' duty, because of a bomb-plot against the Queen in 1887, the Year of Jubilee. He had gone by then, but his eccentric and whimsical use of secret communications and ruses had shown a way to operate beyond the normal limits of police work. At least he had shown that terrorism has to be tackled in ways very different from what he called 'plodding police methods'.

After Jenkinson left, James Monro found himself, in 1887, in charge of both arms of the detectives at the highest level: the CID and the Special 'Secret Department' as it was then known. Monro opened a new section of the CID, with seasoned detectives at the head: Littlechild, Pope, Melville and Quinn. Monro also had a new second-in-command: Robert Anderson was a man who had been working well with intelligence sources in the States. The famous spy 'Henri Caron', alias Thomas Beach from Colchester, was part of the string of agents. This advance in police work was extremely significant: it raised the question of how much the police should know about political activities. After all it was an age of increasing anarchist movements and the growth of militancy in left-wing and Empire groups. Jenkinson had not worried about that too much: he had had Abberline of Ripper fame working for him at one point, checking numbers of immigrants arriving in London. But now all that undercover stuff, in control of one rogue boss such as Jenkinson, would have to stop. The new outfit would have to report to the Home Secretary regularly.

The vindication of the new 'secret office' came with the uncovering of the 'Jubilee Plot' of 1887. The Fenians wanted to place a bomb in Westminster Abbey, to explode during Queen Victoria's attendance at the Thanksgiving service there. Monro's new men were stunningly professional in their detective work, and what they did impinged on espionage. Monro was aware of a man called Millen who was assigned to set up this bombing; the agent Beech had done some excellent work in that respect.

What we then have are two parallel operations of first-rate detective shadowing of suspects. The men in London who were to plant the bomb were living with assumed names but were tracked down and followed. Monro even had an officer assigned to meet Millen in Paris, under the pretence of being 'an interesting invalid' who would chat up Millen and watch him.

Detectives then observed and tracked a man in London known as Melville who turned out to be John J. Morony, a significant figure in the Fenian *Clan-na-Gael*, the American branch. Following that, a certain Harkins was followed and questioned, along with a Mr Callan. The capture of the latter typifies the drama of this episode in detective history. Before the police arrived for him, Callan, said his landlady, had thrown something down the toilet. After a search of the drains, the police found dynamite. It was a magnificent triumph for Monro and his men. But there is an interesting coda: in his memoirs, Anderson claimed that Millen had been a double agent, and that he had been feeding information to London for some years, even during Jenkinson's regime. Whatever the truth of this, the important point is that at the time of the Jubilee, Monro did not know who the conspirators were until help came from beyond his Special Branch.

Even the spy among the Fenians, Major Henri le Caron (Thomas Beach) said in his memoirs:

> As for Millen's connection with the Jubilee explosion, I know very little. The whole undertaking was shrouded in mystery, but it is pretty certain that it was not a *Clan-na-Gael* affair alone. The best description that could be given of it is that it was in its inception a Rossa undertaking financed by *Clan-na-Gael*.

It is one of those affairs that could very easily become a focus of myth and speculation, particularly when we note that the Tsar had agents in Paris and that even the disenchanted former ruler of the Punjab, Duleep Singh, was openly antagonistic to Britain and had meetings with the Imperial Russian ambassador in Paris. The whole situation is ripe for assassination theories and the alignment of suspects from any one of a dozen possible sources.

In practical everyday matters, the point is that in 1886, Special Branch members took the duties of royal protection from A Division and then by 1888 the Branch became known as 'Section D'. It was going to be a force with particular responsibilities for watching the anarchists and the restless émigrés flocking to the East End. It did not take long for them to be generally referred to as the 'Special Branch' – something much more definite and memorable, and also less suspicious, than Section D.

While most attention was being paid to the men who wanted Victoria dead and the British remained terrified of dynamite under the Houses of Parliament, one Henry Seymour was writing in his radical paper 'Anarchist' that the state should be abolished. There were many dissatisfied intellectuals and political eccentrics around London, and although many would be harmless, some had the potential to be very dangerous indeed. The question was (and still is) how might the police differentiate between the two? For instance, in Seven Dials Dan Chatterton wrote a tract called *Chatterton's Commune: The Atheistic Communistic Scorcher* which made him, as Clive Bloom has said, 'a political party of one.' He was, apparently, ' ... a pale haggard old man' who used to 'pour forth wild denunciations of the robbery and injustice that flourishes in our society.' It was to be a typical image. The word 'anarchy' was also to become much misunderstood but its adherents were very closely observed.

The police were dealing with a confused mass of people coping with a still more confused mass of political thought by the closing years of the nineteenth century. Detectives in Special Branch were going to have to deal with the outcome of devious, wayward and often muddled political ideologies swirling around the streets, clubs and pubs under a thousand different names, banners or publications. For the whole of their history, the Metropolitan and City of London police had had to cope with riot, demonstrations and physical assault on officers; now they were to face something more extreme and more sinister, culminating in its first phase in the siege of Sidney Street of 1911. Ranged against the detectives of the Special Branch were now ideologies, marginal mindsets deeply imbued with militancy, and profound dissatisfaction with the status quo.

Before Sidney Street, however, there had been a long history of supposed anarchist behaviour, such as the aims of some to do 'propaganda by the deed' and start bombing campaigns or attempt assassination of dignitaries. Much of this was bluster and bluff, such as the supposed bombings in Walsall in the 1890s, and it involved an *agent provocateur* in the figure of Auguste Coulon. He was an instrument of the workings of the Special Branch and in 1892 there were raids on clubs in both Walsall and London; there were people in possession of Johann Most's book *Revolutionary Warfare* and there were plans to make bombs. A certain David Nicholl was spied on and arrested after Coulon's undercover work.

British anarchists and extreme socialists were largely eccentric and mis-guided, such as the man who fired shots at the Houses of Parliament in broad daylight. But there were dangerous men such as H.B. Samuels and the man who blew himself up in an attempt to create mayhem in Greenwich Park. By the side of these failed and rather pathetic moves to cause a stir, there were the terrorists from abroad, and they were a different matter. These included anarchists and Bolsheviks or Mensheviks and extreme nationalists. These were men who had to carry pistols and use disguise, as they had been dealing with the Ochrana, the secret police in Russia: men who would shoot to kill and ask questions later. In many ways, the experience of coping with these characters would be a steep learning curve for the detectives of Special Branch.

Just across the Channel there had been attempts to murder the French President; the gang responsible fled to Britain and started armed robberies. They were caught after a gun battle in which there were a few casualties, including wounded policemen. But then came the notorious Houndsditch Murders in which an armed gang of Bolsheviks were trapped by some police officers. This was surely a turning point for the Special Branch, because the robbers shot their way out of the trap, killing three constables as they did so. The one man who was shot and wounded, Gardstein, was traced, and slowly the detectives tracked the rest of the gang, finally cornering the last two in Sidney Street. These men were known at the time as Fritz Svaars and 'Yosef'. But as the police closed in tighter and so were seen by the men, one officer was shot dead: the weapons of the terrorists were superior to those of the London police. The Russians had Mausers, capable of accurate fire to 1,000 metres. In a sense, the lesson was learned by means of a sense of failure, because the army had to be called in. The Scots Guards arrived and after a long stand-off the house was set alight. It was a rare spectacle for Londoners: a crowd gathered and even Winston Churchill, the Home Secretary joined in, asking for a double-barrelled shotgun. There is a photograph of him standing amid a crowd of police and troops, some way from the scene of the siege.

The two men were in a flat belonging to Betsy Gershon, 100, Sidney Street. Betsy had been allowed to stay in a lower room, and was not used as a hostage, so police managed to break her free. The first move by the police was in the hands of Inspector Wensley of H Division; it was not a wise move to approach the door and knock. A few shots rang out and the man hit was Detective Leeson, who had to be carried to safety over a roof. Wensley was trapped unarmed, as the gunmen knew where he was but could not make a direct shot at him. Fred Wensley later wrote an account of his experience at the siege, and this is a valuable insight into the detective's part in such an event, but more importantly, it places the siege in the cultural and social setting. Wensley notes that the East End at the time was very violent, and that Russian gangs were at war with each other – the Bessarabians and Odessans. His account of the part played in the community by a detective is a valuable document.

Wensley joined the Metropolitan Police in 1888 and then entered the CID in 1895; he had been a constable during the Ripper enquiries. He wrote his account of the Sidney Street siege at the request of Melville Macnaghten, Assistant Chief Constable of the CID from 1889–91 and Assistant Commissioner for Crime at the time of the siege. Wensley pointed out the difference between the anarchists and the usual gangs: mainly the use of guns rather than knives, but also that they were more professional and seasoned enemies of any state or authority. When Wensley got a lead, linked to the Houndsditch murders, he was keen to follow up. The men killed at Houndsditch had been City of London officers and there was a spirit of vengeance in the air for colleagues. A stranger came to see Wensley – Tomacoff, an informer. He had been placed in a hotel by the CID and was also given plenty of new clothes. His expensive *agent provocateur* work paid off: he knew that 'Yosef' was a close friend of Betty Gershon, and so the hunt was on.

Wensley did try to think things through. He said, 'How were we going to take the men in, without their causing a holocaust among our own police and the population in general that would make the Houndsditch murders look like a picnic?'

Wensley's memoir is a document that defines the changing attitudes of detectives in this kind of work: he noted that a colleague, Mulvaney, wanted to rely on brute force and blast their way into the building. The best plan was to use the geography of the street and box them in. Of course, that gave rise to the question of guns, and Wensley's reflections on that provide the clearest viewpoint of an extremely unusual situation. He said:

> I think it is a mistake for police to carry weapons. I have never carried one or needed one in my whole police career, and I had no wish to encumber myself with one now. But those were exceptional circumstances, and the sad truth was that neither the City Police nor the Met had an armoury that could by any stretch of the imagination be called modern. In H Division we had a few snub-nosed bulldog revolvers, some of which were so antiquated that they had to be reloaded after each shot.

We have to ask, with hindsight, where were the Colt revolvers or similar? But that had never been the way here. It would be more so after that siege, though.

There was even a moment in which the detectives seemed to have borrowed from Sherlock Holmes. Detective Ottaway responded to Macnaghten's idea of making a dummy with enthusiasm, and so it happened. The dummy was placed at a window; his face was brown paper and his body was a hayfork. He was sat as if holding a rifle and, as Macnaghten recalls, 'A fusillade of shots came at once from the house, half a dozen piercing the straw body ... ' But the sensational drama

in Sidney Street and the part played by the detectives was not necessarily what police fiction often calls 'a good result' for the detectives.
The head of the Special Branch at the time, Pat Quinn, was present at
the siege, and Wensley's work helping his colleague over the roof was
commended, but generally, it has to be said that initially they had
blundered in without much thought.

However, the results were mixed: eight other members of the gang
were traced but only four were charged; police were up against all kinds
of barriers in the strategies of the gang members to protect their own.
The woman at the heart of the case, Nina Vassileva, involved at the core
of the outfit, had her sentence quashed on appeal.

Prominent and dramatic cases like this appeared, to some, to confirm
the often expressed view that the value of the detective branch is a
drop in the ocean and that we were naïve in comparison with many
European nations in our detective work with regard to political contexts. What the Houndsditch murders and the siege of Sidney Street
did, if nothing else, was make the presence of anarchists and terrorists
more acknowledged, more a part of the scene. This was largely due to
the mediation of the anarchist by means of individual villains as well as
of stereotype bombers. The clearest example is that of Peter Piatkow,
known as 'Peter the Painter', whose photograph was posted around
London; yet it seems that Peter fled to Russia where he was supposed to
have become a Cheka member.

Of course, there was something else going on, equally political and
just as important for the detectives in London: the fear of German spies,
just a few years before Sidney Street, and of course, into the years of the
Great War. As Churchill was standing with his shotgun at Sidney Street,
Captain Vernon Kell of the South Staffordshire Regiment was in the
intelligence service and found himself doing very much what spymaster
Jenkinson had done twenty years before – create a team of agents. One
of his key men was retired detective William Melville (known as 'M').
Melville hailed from County Kerry and had joined the Metropolitan
Police in 1872. He was one of the first men in the Special Irish Branch
and up until 1903 (when he resigned) he had been an expert on the

1 Sir Richard Mayne, one of the first
Police Commissioners

2 Superintendent Williamson

3 Chief Inspector Nat Druscovich

4 Townsend, Bow Street Runner
and bodyguard to George III

5 Colquhoun's *Treatise* title page

6 Inspector Field confronted with
an unexpected clue

Left: 7 Detective Abberline, a key man on the Jack the Ripper cases

Below: 8 Scalby Manor, Scarborough – home of the bloodhounds used in the Ripper hunt

Scalby Manor

ATTEMPT
To Assassinate
THE QUEEN
And PRINCE ALBERT.

Yesterday evening as her Majesty & Prince Albert were taking their evening ride in an open carriage, about six o'clock, & when they had proceeded a little way up Constitution Hill, a man who was standing on the side next to the Green Park, took a pistol from his breast & fired it at her Majesty. The Prince, who probably observed the action of the man, placed his hand behind her Majesty's head & pressed it forward, to which, under Providence, her preservation may be owing. The man immediately fired another pistol, but happily with as little effect. The Prince directed the carriage to proceed as if nothing had happened. The villain who made this diabolical attempt was seized by a number of persons who rushed towards him, & on the arrival of the police he was taken to Queen Square Office. Her Majesty rose in the carriage immediately after the discharge of the first pistol, and the second was fired as rapidly as if it had been the second shot in a duel. The reports of both pistols were very loud.

The indignation expressed by the surrounding gentry, and, indeed, all parties who had heard of the nefarious attempt, was most unequivocally expressed. There was an immense number of horsemen and carriages drawn up in the Park, extending from the statue of Achilles to the Park, and her Majesty as she approached, the most lively and loyal cheering was manifested, and the air was literally rent with enthusiastic shouts and greetings.

FURTHER PARTICULARS.

On being taken to the station-house, he gave his name EDWARD OXFORD, a native of Birmingham, 17 years of age, and lived as pot-boy at the Hog-in-the-Pound, Mary-le-Bone Lane, facing Oxford Street, and that he had a room at No. 6, West Street, West Square, on searching of which the police found a sword and a black crape cap made to fit the face, a powder flask and bullets which fitted the pistol's.

The prisoner will be examined this day at the Home Office.

BIRT, Printer, 39, Great St. Andrew Street, Seven Dials.

9 Article reporting the attempt to assassinate the Queen

10 James J. Thomson, one of the first professionals in London

THE "ROOKERY," ST. GILES'S, 1850.

11 'The Rookery', St Giles. Den of villains

THE OLD HOUSE OF DETENTION, CLERKENWELL.

12 House of Detention,
Clerkenwell

13 Dublin Castle, Jenkinson's base
against Fenians

Above: 14 Sherbourne Hotel, Dublin. Where Jenkinson recruited his agents

Left: 15 Thomas Holmes, police court documentarist and source of valuable information

Detective Stories Gone Wrong.

The Adventures of Sherlaw Kombs.

By Luke Sharp.

Illustrated by George Hutchinson.

(With apologies to Dr. Conan Doyle, and his excellent book, "A Study in Scarlet.")

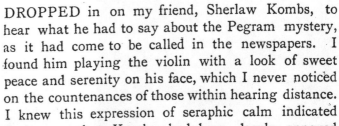

DROPPED in on my friend, Sherlaw Kombs, to hear what he had to say about the Pegram mystery, as it had come to be called in the newspapers. I found him playing the violin with a look of sweet peace and serenity on his face, which I never noticed on the countenances of those within hearing distance. I knew this expression of seraphic calm indicated that Kombs had been deeply annoyed about something. Such, indeed, proved to be the case, for one of the morning papers had contained an article eulogising the alertness and general competence of Scotland Yard. So great was Sherlaw Kombs's contempt for Scotland Yard that he never would visit Scotland during his vacations, nor would he ever admit that a Scotchman was fit for anything but export.

He generously put away his violin, for he had a sincere liking for me, and greeted me with his usual kindness.

"I FOUND HIM PLAYING THE VIOLIN."

"I have come," I began, plunging at once into the matter on my mind, "to hear what you think of the great Pegram mystery."

"I haven't heard of it," he said quietly, just as if all London were not talking of that very thing. Kombs was curiously ignorant on some subjects, and abnormally learned on others. I found, for instance, that political discussion with him was impossible, because he did not know who Salisbury and Gladstone were. This made his friendship a great boon.

"The Pegram mystery has baffled even Gregory, of Scotland Yard."

"I can well believe it," said my friend, calmly. "Perpetual

17 Detectives and constables at the Moat Farm murder. (Back row, from left to right: Constables Field and Lindsey; front row: Sergeant Scott and Constable Fell)

18 Gustav Steinhauer, the Kaiser's Master Spy. Vernon Kell and Detective Quinn were pitted against him

Dr. Crippin.

Right: 19 Dr Crippin

Below: 20 Hilldrop Crescent, Crippin's house where Belle's body was found

Left: 21 Inspector Walter Dew, the man who arrested Crippin

Below: 22 London and North East detectives at Kings Cross in the 1940s

Above: 23 A hypothetical investigation at Hendon Detective Training. As part of 'X's' training, he is shown the relics of past crimes.

Right: 24 A plaster mould is made of impressions found at the foot of the office fire escape. The cast prepared from this mould exactly reproduces the footprints. By this method a permanent record is obtained for later examination

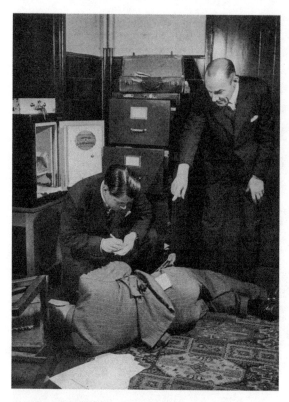

25 First move by pupil 'X' is to take full details of the crime, noting in particular the position of the dead man and the state of the clothing

26 The hypothetical case opens. 'X' is taken to the 'body' of a victim of a hit-and-run driver. 'X' questions a witness, who describes a car which passed at the time. Unfortunately the man failed to observe its number

political émigrés in London, running what was called 'counter refugee operations'. He was certainly a very capable Scotland Yard man, not at all an Inspector Lestrade; his skill in establishing a network of informers and agents was just what Kell at MI5 wanted. His most famous connection is surely in his links with Sigmund Rosenblum ('Reilly – Ace of Spies').

Kell's activities were to show the way for the new Special Branch men; he had learned from them, via Melville, but was now to succeed so amazingly in tracking down German spies that he would be a useful man in all kinds of ways. By 1914, Kell and his network had located every German spy in England. His men had even been watching D.H. Lawrence in Cornwall, as he had a German wife. But more seriously, on the day that war with Germany was declared, twenty-one people were arrested by English and Scottish police. Some were reprieved, but a number were executed.

In the early years of the twentieth century then, professional detectives in London were working for CID or with the Special Branch. Private detectives were still very much divorce men, though there were those small-scale private agencies doing very well in other ways, influenced by the great Scottish-American Pinkerton and William J. Burns, correspondent of Conan Doyle. Whatever the status of the detective, the Edwardian period gave us the fictional sleuth in abundance. In fact, so great was the level of interest in Holmes and his rivals in the popular novels and stories of the time that detective work was depicted as glamorous and exciting; no doubt it was when there was a siege on or a villain to tail and corner. But there were other revolutions in the trade going on, and many of these were scientific rather than street-based work.

What was to happen when Scotland Yard became a base for forensics, as well as common sense and following the 'nose', was that we were to have an increase in demand for the Yard detective going out of the city to help in the regions. In 1903 a few things happened at the Yard that typified the new age: a private telephone line was put into use at Central Office; Sir Edward Henry became Commissioner (one of the very best ever); and the Women's Social and Political Union was founded in Manchester by Emmeline and Christabel Pankhurst.

In the new century, detectives were destined to use the benefits of fingerprints in one context, and to watch and follow suffragettes in another, amongst other novelties in their always challenging profession. Science and discretion were to go hand in hand: the sleuth was to be an all-rounder now, with demands made of all his qualities by all kinds of citizens, criminals and otherwise.

It seems symbolic of the revolution in detective work that took place in the period between *c.*1890 and 1910, that during the Ripper panic and the constant criticism of the detective officers in the press, that Sir Charles Warren should be attracted to the idea of bringing in bloodhounds. The artist Louis Wain drew a sketch of Warren trotting across a field with bloodhounds sniffing 'in full cry' and looking lost ('at fault'). The irony was that, not long after, Inspector Abberline asked for some bloodhounds but none were available. One newspaper wrote that 'the animals have bolted and have not been recovered.' It somehow typifies the backward-looking earnestness of the detectives before they were really pressed into making the CID far more streamlined and efficient than was initially envisaged.

But there was more endeavour and enterprise in the bloodhounds story than the paper realised: Warren had obtained them from the Scalby Manor kennels near Scarborough, from the breeder, Edwin Brough. Bloodhounds Barnaby and Burgho came south and performed their duties in Hyde Park, and yet were thought to be too easy-going for such tough work. The Metropolitan Police decided not to buy Burgho and the notion was dropped.

It took a long time for radical changes to set in. The note about the antiquated firearms of H Division by Wensley says it all: over twenty years had passed since the Ripper year and yet the Peel-ite concept of the constable on the beat was fundamentally the same; the detective officers were undergoing a similar trajectory in their time.

8

THE NEW SLEUTHS: PROFESSIONALS AND AMATEURS

One of the most celebrated detectives of the twentieth century, Fred Cherrill ('Cherrill of the Yard') explained his early fascination with fingerprints by telling the tale of his going to an old mill with his father in a storm. The miller was ill and someone was needed to grind the corn to meet demand. In the mill, flour was sprayed everywhere, putting a white film over every surface, and young Fred found himself grabbing an eel his father threw across the room at him, with orders to put it in a sack. His hands were caked in eel slime and then he writes,

> Startled, I put out a hand to steady myself. For just a moment my slime-covered fingers rested on the wooden chute, which had become highly polished by all the flour and meal which had passed over its surface … I was gazing at the chute in awed fascination … There, by the agency of nature alone, were my fingerprints!

Cherrill's story accounts for the long history of the knowledge of fingerprints, long before they were used in forensics. There had been various academics who had done work on prints but nothing had come of it: a professor at the University of Breslau in 1823 had read a Latin thesis on fingerprints in a lecture; and the artist Thomas Bewick had made wood engravings of fingerprints, using them as identifying signatures on his works. In China, for many centuries, thumb-prints had been used in documents for identity purposes in ratification. Similarly, these impressions had been used in India with illiterate members of the population; when the scientist Francis Galton got to work on the subject, he wrote a book-length study, simply called *Fingerprints*, published in 1892. In some ways, the introduction of fingerprinting into police work is similar to the rivalry to reach the South Pole: while Sir Edward Henry was using fingerprints in India for crime investigation, the same work was being done in Argentina by Francesca Rojas. But once Henry had introduced fingerprinting into the repertoire of detection methods at the Yard, it was to cause a revolution in detective procedure.

The prototype scenario and first conviction by the use of prints came in 1902 when the Yard had around one-hundred fingerprints in their first small volume of records. It was a murder case, and it took place at Chapman's Oil and Colour Stores in Deptford. An old couple, Thomas and Ann Farrow, ran the shop and they had an assistant, young William Jones. Along with Louis Kidman, Jones found Thomas's corpse and later the still breathing Ann Farrow.

The old man had been brutally beaten, having a broken cheekbone and a fractured skull; the doctor said that the man had died around ninety minutes earlier. Once Ann Farrow had been taken to hospital and the scene was ready for some inspection, Chief Inspector Fred Fox arrived with two photographers to do his work. Crime scene investigation, in something close to the modern sense, was being born that day. No less a figure than Melville Macnaghten came to assist and then took charge. The killer had not forced entry: that was the first important detail established. There had been a frenzied search of the whole shop and house, but the scene suggested that after going upstairs and hitting Mrs Farrow, the suspect had come downstairs and then fought the old man again, as he had recovered from the first blow.

There were no witnesses; three masks were found abandoned in the shop so now Macnaghten knew he was looking for three killers, and that made the murder all the more savage and reprehensible. There was no indication as to what weapon had been used in the murderous attacks either. The question now on the detective's mind was whether Ann Farrow would recover and give descriptions. What was particularly unhelpful in the course of the usual tracing procedure in pawn shops and similar outlets was that the killers had only taken money. That created a dead end in the normal line of enquiry. It was looking desperate for the Chief; another shopkeeper had been killed in London the same day. Then, the final blow: Mrs Farrow died.

Macnaghten went back to the bloodbath that was the sitting room of the Farrow household. Casting his eye across the room and the pools of blood, he thought of the surface prints that had just been used in smaller-scale arrests. Would the Farrow murder be the first opportunity to try this new device? He established that none of the police personnel at the shop had touched the cashbox, and then he covered his fingers with a handkerchief and showed his team the print on the box. Collins, of the new Fingerprint Branch, was a sleuth with a scientific bent; he had been working on other types of basic forensics and was excited about this new technique. It was a matter of magnifying glasses and intense study at that time; he had a small collection of filed prints from known criminals and that was it. There had been a long-established method of filing basic records of habitual offenders, so there was some hope of a 'result'. But the print on the cash box had no match in Collins' shelves.

Basic police work, however, provided the lead that would eventually take the investigation back to the cashbox. A milkman at work on the day of the killing had seen two men leaving the shop and he gave a description of them. The milkman saw that they had left the door open and told them so but they took no notice as they said there was someone behind them. To tally with this, three men had been seen in a local pub very early that day – and they answered the descriptions. It was when a certain Ellen Stanton came forward that things accelerated; she had seen two men running at the right time, and they had the same appearance as the two suspects, and Ellen knew one of them. Macnaghten was now searching for one Alfred Stratton. The man was taken in Deptford. The identification parade failed, but Collins took the prints of Stratton and his brother. One print matched that of Alfred.

What happened next set a pattern for almost all succeeding scientific forensic advances when it came to the implementation of knowledge and its part in the court process. In other words, this new detective force, with its fingerprints and other types of records, was going to find it hard to convince judge and jury about the new methods of detection. But the Stratton brothers went to the gallows; hangman John Billington officiated at Wandsworth. The judge, Mr Justice Channell, had said in court that the men should not be convicted on fingerprint evidence alone and that was the case. But the first trial involving fingerprint evidence had happened. From that point on the concept would be a little more familiar, and the newspapers played their part to ensure that.

What happened in the closing years of the nineteenth century and the first years of the new century was that Scotland Yard began to acquire a much more sophisticated records department than ever before and fingerprints began to play a major part in that. Edward Henry initiated the Central Fingerprint Bureau and together with the Register of Habitual Criminals, the Criminal Records Office was created. Three CID men, Stedman, Collins and Hunt, were to run the new section.

Fred Cherrill's memoirs give us an insight into what the Fingerprint Bureau was like in its early days; he joined it in 1920, when it was in the old part of Scotland Yard. Cherrill was working, in his early years, with the same format of records that had existed fifteen years before. These were various anthropometric sources and he was very critical of this 'chest of drawers': 'The intrinsic value was nil. But to me it had more than a little sentimental appeal.' It was, in fact, the basic product of the system begun by Alphonse Bertillon (1853–1914) who had been a worker in the Paris Prefecture of Police records department. *Bertillonage* became the method of classification by 'mugshot' as he had been interested in using photography for recording purposes. His '*portrait parle*' became a standard concept in visual records of criminals. He was opposed to fingerprinting and thought that photographs were the better means of identification. He had worked out that the chances of two people of similar profiles being exactly the same height were four to one. He extended this to all areas of dimensions in all parts of the frame and so produced a template for individualising the subject. If the subject were to be a criminal, then think of the value of that in the detective's records.

His similar work on facial characteristics was the forerunner of the identikit, and his methods did have some success, notably in the case of an anarchist called Ravachol. But the limitations were exposed in the case of twins called Fox; his methods could not differentiate between them and this was to allow fingerprinting to take the lead in that area of forensics. It must have seemed to some that detective work was being passed to the scientists. But the theoretical work being done in the first decades of the twentieth century was often far removed from everyday detective work. Such developments as Victor Balthazard's study of hair was perhaps an exception, as his knowledge of human hair helped to convict the murderer of Germaine Bichon. But other work, such as haemoglobin tests and antibody tests on blood, were going on within academia.

Yet the impact of science was destined to be profound. The Departmental Committee on Detective Work of 1938 led to greater clarity with regard to the place of science in police work; this report registered the fact that the more advanced skills needed by detective officers tended to widen the gap between uniformed men and plain clothes. After that momentous report, a completely new attitude to detective training emerged that set up proper training, which was to include some knowledge of what forensics involved. The Metropolitan Police set up their first truly professional laboratory in 1935 and others followed in the regions, notably in Nottingham, Cardiff and Birmingham throughout the 1930s. There was to be a national unit dealing with forensic science as well.

By the late 1940s the place of science in the detective training curriculum was well established. A *Daily Express* documentary led by Percy Hoskins, revealed to the public the state of the art at the time. Hoskins noted, 'Scotland Yard does not expect its men to be scientists. But it does insist that they become fully conversant with the resources of the modern forensic science laboratory, and the aid it can give in establishing guilt or innocence.' Hoskins summarised the resources available. The laboratory around 1950 could cope with areas such as dust, hair, fibres and bloodstains; they could analyse handwriting and study abrasions on car paintwork. They had also been busy with increasing police knowledge of burglar's tools and methods. It was clearly common practice in detective training to teach men what was done by the scientists, so that no blunders would be made at the scene of crime.

Hoskins even gives an example of a case of sabotage in the Second World War in which carpets were analysed as scientists searched for particles of dust that would have chemicals used by the bombers adhered to them; those findings were then related to the same inspection of suspects' clothing and arrests were made. Everything was being extended from the basic notion of 'every contact leaves evidence' principle and refinements of that went on having an impact as the century advanced. It was a period in which the forensic specialists, and the celebrated pathologist Dr Keith Simpson, came into prominence. A typical case study that explains the progress made in applying science to crime is that of 'The Wigwam Girl' of 1942.

The body of a girl was found out on Hankley Common twenty miles from London. Detectives found only what Hoskins called 'a rag and a bone and a hank of hair.' The girl was Joan Wolfe, a nineteen-year-old convent girl who had taken to a wandering life around Godalming. She began to remind observers of a native-American and was seen with American soldiers. The nickname stuck. Then, in October 1942 some soldiers working at a beauty spot known as the Devil's Punchbowl found her body and the first responses suggested that it had been a ritual killing.

A murder squad led by Chief Superintendent Greeno went to work on the case. It was going to be a difficult challenge because the girl's body was severely decomposed. But Simpson was brought in and his first discovery was that she had had blonde hair. Local appeals for information led to the identification of the body as that of 'The Wigwam Girl'. A makeshift woodland dwelling was found nearby, hence her nickname and identity were almost certainly known. As enquiries extended, a cricket pavilion was located in which she had previously lived and it was there that detectives found some writing on the walls. Also found was a letter from the girl's mother, and so police then had a name for the dead girl.

The case became one of the first enquiries in which teams of specialists were brought in to do all kinds of scene of crime study, including analysis of hairs on branches and the use of an army mine-detector to find materials that were buried. But the science was not all that mattered: there was a name on the pavilion wall – August Sangret, French-Canadian and half Cree, who, when interviewed, talked about his relationship with Joan. The girl had been killed by being battered with a branch of birch, and the scientists had reconstructed her smashed skull. It was then that old-fashioned detective work came into play: a series of hypothetical events had to be imagined leading to the girl's battering. She had been stabbed before death and that helped this reconstruction of events. In the end, it came down to the fact that Greeno and his team needed the knife and only determined and relentless searches finally led to its discovery in a drain of Sangret's camp. It was a very distinctive blade, curved like a parrot's beak, and so other people recalled it in Sangret's possession.

Also, by 1950 the science of ballistics had advanced considerably, all based on the fact that no two weapons can produce identical bullet markings; test bullets from suspected murder weapons were being used then as a matter of course. Even cartridge casings had a 'fingerprint' individuality. But during the first half of the twentieth century, ballistics was more complex than one might imagine and even the leading experts could be challenged, as in the case of Robert Churchill when he was called in to help solve the puzzle of a death in Lincolnshire in 1931. Retired Metropolitan Police officer George Kitchen had a farm at Gedney that he worked with his two sons. One morning, George and his son James came outside to work and James propped his gun, loaded, by a barn. As they cleaned their spades, James's dog, Prince, came out and from that point it is unclear whether or not the dog knocked the gun over and caused it to fire, or whether Kitchen shot his son. The fact was that James was shot and no-one else was present.

Halland, Chief Constable of Lincolnshire, was involved in the enquiry and of course he needed an opinion about the ballistics. Could the gun have been accidentally fired? Did the angle of entry of the bullet into

James' body correlate with the position of the gun? George was arrested and charged but Sir Bernard Spilsbury and then Churchill were called in to add their expertise. Spilsbury's post mortem showed that the wounds were caused from above, then downwards and forwards. In other words, the likelihood was that the gun had been fired by someone from the hip or shoulder. Another expert, Mr Paling, confirmed that this was the likely account of the firing, suggesting also that, as the wound had fractured two ribs, the shot had come from an angle of fifty-five degrees. His tests indicated that when the gun was fired the muzzle must have been about a yard from the victim. He stressed that 'the gun could only have been fired by human agency.'

Then, enter Robert Churchill. He was of a prestigious standing in the world of shooting and gun-making and had worked with detectives on several major cases. His shop, close to the National Gallery in Trafalgar Square, had a cellar in which he conducted tests with firearms when he was working for the police. Everyone involved in the workings of the criminal law as a professional knew and respected Churchill's work. But what was to happen in the Kitchen case opened up all kinds of lessons for the detective branch to learn from, mainly in terms of procedure when forensics were involved in a murder case. Churchill had actually visited the Kitchens' farm and he had been sure that the gun could not have been fired by the dog knocking it over. He said that 'the pull required to discharge the left barrel was so heavy that I was able to lift the gun at full cock off the ground with my finger hooked round the trigger, without releasing the action.' With this kind of certainty, it is amazing to learn that subsequent events almost wrecked the man's career, and the spin-off story of Churchill and the accusation that he had interfered with the gun (and therefore the evidence) is almost as sensational as the trial itself.

Churchill took the gun to his London laboratory. Here he found that it would require a mean pressure of seven pounds on the trigger to shoot it. This was fully two pounds of pressure heavier than the normal pull. In his typically thorough way, Churchill used tests in which a series of shots were fired at steel and leather from varying distances. He was certain, after all his work, that the wounds that killed young James could not have been self-inflicted. He also agreed with Spilsbury that the wound could not have been inflicted by a freak accident, such as the weapon being knocked over by a dog. It was after his written report based on these tests was delivered that George Kitchen was arrested in Lincolnshire.

The case was to demonstrate to the detectives investigating in the provinces (as they so often did) that their main problems would arise in court: something that was a lesson for the future. The clash between the use of experts of an amateur status and the general sense of investigation among the ranks of the detectives, was to prove difficult for some time, and was only improved when the Yard's own laboratory was set up. Churchill and his evidence were put against Sir Sydney Smith by the defence counsel, and so began a confrontation of scientific experts. Sergeant Lown in Gedney accused Churchill of interfering with the gun during his test and that was the beginning of the legal problem. From that point, Churchill was being tried, as well as Kitchen. Major Burrard reported to the Home Secretary that Churchill had interfered with the gun and Churchill replied to this very serious charge:

> The lock was in this state when I returned it to the Old Bailey and I honestly believe that these witnesses have made a mistake ... I repeat that if anything had happened to this gun, to my knowledge I would have told you so. I have given evidence as a gun expert for you for nearly 22 years and never before has expert evidence been called against me.

He was exonerated and in the trial at the Old Bailey a point was reached at which Prince, the dog, appeared on a table while the action of his rather strong tail was discussed; could that tail have smacked against the trigger? It was farcical, and George Kitchen was acquitted. There was no resolution to the case and the truth will never be known. But as far as detectives pursuing a case were concerned, it raised the issue of expert testimony and scientific evidence. If such a well-known and respected ballistics expert could be called into question, then anyone could.

But the 'science of detection' is not only evident in the laboratory. The logistics of running a detective branch entails much more than theory and experiment. In London and across the country the networks of gang crime, together with the increasingly brutal and ruthless robberies and killings in the streets after the Great War, when so many men acted desperately in an age of mass unemployment and deprivation, meant that the Yard needed new strategies. Most notable of all the initiatives taken by the 'new men' in the ranks was the Flying Squad. This was formed in 1919 specifically to combat that flood of crime after the war. The idea was that a small centralised body of officers would work in particular areas, each under the direction of a Superintendent. The central concept was another variation on the use of an independent unit, working with its own methods, set apart from mainstream policing. At first, horse-drawn wagons with spy-holes had been used (hired from the Great Western Railway) but then these were replaced by two Crossley tenders and then on to vehicles much more speedy. Before the Great War, detectives had the measure of the criminal geography of the metropolis; it has been claimed that in 1910 around 95% of crooks operating in London and the Home Counties were known to Yard officers. There was also a well-established network of informants and a rapport was made that would create immediate lines of enquiry when a crime was committed. Only after the Second World War was a directive given, signalling a change of attitude in the top brass. Detectives were forbidden, according to Stanley Firmin, to 'have any truck with crooks or others living on the fringe of crookdom and ordered under threat of dire penalties to discontinue at once their visits to those places where crooks were likely to congregate.' When a fresh crime wave, fronted by many new faces, began there was a serious problem. Many villains were ex-servicemen who had adapted their military skills to activities on the wrong side of the law.

The epidemic of crime expressed itself as armed robbery. The squad assembled to combat this had to have a number of expert drivers, and men with other particular talents. The first force consisted of 180 CID men, and there were branches of the Squad at five locations around London. Smaller squads of a dozen men were the staple of the work, and this group included a mix of sergeants and constables. The first name given to this famous cadre of men was The Mobile Patrol Experiment, used until 1920, but thereafter known as the Flying Squad. The force was constantly streamlined in the next decade and by 1929 it was given an establishment of forty officers, led by a Detective Superintendent of C1, Central CID.

After the Second World War it became known as Branch C8. Once the Crossley tenders had been brought in to replace the horse and wagon, the next innovation was a radio transmitting station placed on the roof of Scotland Yard, using Morse code. By 1927 new cars came in: Lea Francis convertibles with a top speed of 75mph. Brooklands motor track was used to train the special drivers who would work with the Squad and their cars became known as Q Cars because of their interchangeable number plates. But after the new cars had suffered badly by the ramming of villains' vehicles, a sturdier yet still fast car was brought in, the Invictas, with a top speed of 90mph.

Most notable in the work of the Flying Squad was the way they related to the old school crooks, the ones who resented the amoral and gun-centred antics of the new breed of villain. The 'career criminals' were more likely to become informants and develop a rapport with the Squad officers who regularly worked their territory. As this paid dividends for the Squad in its high clear-up rates in their work, that system suited all parties very well.

The Squad was the most suitable counter measure against a particularly nasty and desperate racetrack war that went on in the 1920s, principally involving gangs from different parts of the country. After the Great War, racetrack bookmakers provided easy money for protection racket crooks. Billy Kimber was a main player, leading the Birmingham Boys gang; they had an alliance with the Leeds Gang and as time went on, their main enemies became the Sabini brothers from Clerkenwell. Kimber was based in London, so his rival Charles 'Dardy' Sabini was not far away from him. When Sabini and his four brothers looked towards the racetrack for a regular income, there was bound to be trouble. The two outfits would be taking each other on, and it was up to the detectives of the Flying Squad to prevent trouble whenever they could.

In 1921 there was a major confrontation after the Derby. At the track, Detective Inspector Stevens was there to observe the two factions, so they decided to meet elsewhere. On the road from Epsom, there was a blunder: the Leeds Crowd, friends of the Kimber men, were attacked on the assumption that they were Sabini's men. There was a bloody fight at Ewell and Stevens rushed to the scene. A charabanc used by the attackers was spotted parked by a public house and the police took away the spark plugs before cornering the villains. The hero of the hour was Sergeant Dawson, who faced the whole gang and as they came at him, he pulled out a revolver and said he would shoot the first man who tried to escape.

Of course, Sabini had come out well, because his enemies had mistakenly attacked each other. But matters were still extremely serious in the gang wars; there were murders in 1924, and a crowd of racing thugs attacked a police officer at Victoria station. The protection racket was thriving; by the mid-1920s a bookmaker was not safe unless he paid at least £20 a day to the crooks. After a particularly vicious confrontation, the Flying Squad was given a direct brief to take on the gangs more aggressively. At this point a detective of considerable fame appeared on the scene – Fred 'Nutty' Sharpe. He was a tough rugby player from South Wales who had been hardened working down the pit. He began his police career as a constable in London, working in the East End. After being spotted as a likely candidate by the CID chief Wensley, Sharpe was assigned to the Flying Squad and this decision was the right one.

Sharpe was tough and fearless. All varieties of crooks at the tracks were his prey, from muggers to pickpockets. Tales were told of his pretending to be a drunk in order to attract robbers, and then he would take them on with his fists. As writer Dick Kirby has said, 'Only the most reckless of gang members would refuse to obey his command. The first to attempt recalcitrance, either by word or deed, would find himself flat on his back, nursing a broken jaw, courtesy of Nutty.'

As was common practice, Squad specialists were called to help outside the city as well, but it was on the tracks that they were in demand, and this continued for decades. Most famous of all was the episode of the Hoxton Mob in 1936, when some bookies linked to the Sabini gang were brutally attacked by Hoxton members. Nutty Sharpe heard of the plan and he was there at the course; most of the perpetrators were taken to trial and sentenced, some sentences being three years. This was at Lewes Assizes, and it marked the victory of the Squad over the gangs on the tracks. Sharpe became head of the Squad for a short period before his retirement in July 1937. The one statement that best sums up that hard and intelligent officer is his comment on the secret of accurate knowledge: 'The more crooks a man knows intimately, the more he knows about the underworld and what it is thinking and doing, then the more likely he is to be of use.'

The inter-war years for detective work were largely a time when several practical aids and innovations came into use, even down to the introduction of the 'murder bag' by Sir Bernard Spilsbury. This bag contained the various items needed at the scene of crime of a murder. Spilsbury and Chief Inspector Percy Savage had had to handle the flesh of a body in decomposition and this brought home to Spilsbury the need for officers to use rubber gloves to avoid sepsis. From that detail, a whole panoply of protective items was introduced.

More significant was the increasing sophistication in the use of the press and general media by detectives. In the nineteenth century, the police publication *Hue and Cry* had listed wanted suspects or known criminals. The press were used more and more in order to utilise the public in investigations, and when radio was established there were even more possibilities. In 1933 there was the very first public appeal in an attempt to track down a killer. This was Samuel Furnace, who had killed Walter Spatchett in Camden Town. Not until 1953 could the public see a wanted man's face on a television screen, though the press had always been adept at providing line drawings of suspects, as well as of victims. But in 1948 there was a murder hunt that exemplifies the use of the press by staff involved in a detection process. The case was that of a plain-clothes officer, P.C. Edgar, who had been at work in a team that aimed to track down some burglars in Highgate. Edgar stopped a man at Wade's Hill to ask him some questions. He wrote a few details in his notebook, but was then murdered. It was rare for a constable to be shot and to die of wounds, and so there was public outrage. However, there was a vital clue – the name Thomas Donald of Enfield was written in the notebook.

The detective on the case, DI Thomas Stinton, wanted to use a newspaper appeal. There had only been a Public Information Officer at the Yard since 1945: Percy Fearnley. Stinton and Fearnley carefully worded the appeal for information. It was known that a certain Donald George Thomas was a deserter from the army and the appeal was 'The police urgently wish to interview Donald George Thomas, who was believed to be able to help them in their enquiries.' This led to a response from a man who said that his wife was missing and that it was very likely that she was with Thomas. A photograph of the woman, Noreen Winkless, was in the papers and there was a quick response from a landlady who had seen her. There was a scene of high drama worthy of any detective thriller when Inspector Moody and a constable went to the address. There they found Thomas; they struggled with him and stopped him from grabbing his revolver. When caught and restrained, the killer said, 'That gun's full up and they were all for you, you bastards.'

When Basil Dean's famous film about the Metropolitan Police, *The Blue Lamp*, was made in 1949, the liaison between detectives and media was complete. At the same time, newspapers and magazines began to take an interest in the work done by detectives. Percy Hoskin's book *No Hiding Place* (1950) provided a very rare item: a documentary insight with dozens of photographs of detective work, from forensics to scene of crime procedure.

Also in the inter-war years, somewhat in the shadow of the police professionals, were the private investigators. One of the most overworked institutions in the first half of the twentieth century was arguably the Probate, Divorce and Admiralty Division in the English legal system. John Mortimer describes this with the benefit of direct experience, as he started as a barrister in 1940 when a marriage could only really be terminated with the evidence of a serious breach of the vows being available, most typically adultery but also extreme cruelty. Mortimer explains:

> Admiralty cases … where seafaring men arrived unrolling charts, were closed books to us and called for specialist lawyers … Divorce was sexier, more dramatic and supplied our daily bread, so that I was housed, fed, watered, clothed and educated almost entirely on the proceeds of adultery, cruelty and wilful neglect to provide reasonable maintenance.

The same theory of economic survival could be applied to the private detective. It was a business that thrived and the newspapers in the period from after the Great War to the 1960s are full of stories that enlighten the historian with regard to this shady business of sleuthing for adultery. It was also a business in which women detectives were beginning to be used more often. From the 1916 Police Act and the 1928 Lee Commission, women had increasingly played parts in police work and gradually, women detectives were also part of the teams, usually as aides, in this period. In 1920 General Horwood, Metropolitan Police Commissioner, made it clear that women in the force were about to be more widely employed, and he hinted that women detectives would be figures integrated into general detective work. He noted, 'There is now a system of interchanging information with regard to criminals which, when fully developed, should go far to overcome some of the chief difficulties with which detectives have now to contend.' In the professional police, the days of women detectives were to arrive when the Ghost Squads were operating against robber-gangs and fraud outfits a little later.

For private detectives, sleuthing in hotels observing adultery was a lucrative and interesting career option. It was often so difficult to obtain a divorce that people did what one of Mortimer's clients did: adopt a disguise and pretend to be the adulterous husband in the hotel, and then have a detective photograph him in action. Moreover, often the work of detectives in such cases was stranger than fiction. In the case of variety agent William Henshall in 1918 we find a typical story. Henshall petitioned for divorce on the grounds of adultery which followed an initial suit based on her cruelty. Henshall was a gambler and a variety agent and producer. He existed on the fringe of popular variety, and his most celebrated success was the show *The Sugar Baby*. He married an actress, Jean Allistone, but this became, in the words of the judge, 'of a violent nature that was almost incredible. The history of the married life was alternate passion and quarrels, violence and reconciliation.'

The couple had caused disgraceful scenes at the Waldorf Hotel. On one occasion, Jean punched William; on another they had a noisy row in the foyer. Jean was heard to threaten William with 'a jolly good hiding' and was also heard to say that she had met a young man she loved much better than William. Incredibly, William employed three female detectives to take on the task of proving his wife's adultery. They noted that she was in the habit of meeting young men, particularly officers, at the Savoy and at Murray's Club. Then she had apparently gone down on her knees and asked to be taken back.

On one occasion, William appears to have had a good time joining his detective team; he accompanied them in a cab as they began to trail Jean on one of her assignations. But William admitted in court that he was not beyond reproach. He was asked why his licence to be an agent had been withdrawn and agreed that it was because he was not 'a man of proper moral character.' But the detectives had no trouble in filling their notebooks with evidence of Jean's improper behaviour.

Some of the detective work undertaken by the private gumshoes was bold in the extreme. A woman detective on one assignment boarded with the woman she was watching to prove adultery, and the victim was so convinced by the detective's 'front' that she wrote to her, describing her life: 'Dear Mrs Smith … It was not to be expected that I continue my lonely wretched existence in cheap boarding houses and there was always a certain amount of ignominy in my position …' She unloaded her private feelings to 'Mrs Smith.'

Of course, private investigators could and did overstep the mark and become criminals themselves. In 1919 Michael Johnson was given six month's hard labour after two Scotland Yard men observed him take a suitcase from a luggage van at King's Cross. A stolen chequebook was also on his person. That kind of incident was not rare. On the other hand, the sleuths' crimes could be farcical, and all a part of their bizarre lifestyle. One event in 1920 involved two police detectives arresting a crooked private detective who was threatening a barrister. Major E.H. Coombe, received a letter from an investigator called John Winter, demanding £50. Coombe called in the detectives, and two officers hid themselves in the chambers. Winter arrived and asked for his money, saying, 'Have you got my money? You have done me once.'

Coombe shouted, 'Officers!' and the two Yard men entered the room. But Winter's aggressive attitude had prompted the barrister to take out a pistol. 'This is not a case for arms!' Winter said. It turned out that Winter was a special constable, of German descent. He had a bundle of threatening letters on him when taken. His detective work was a way into working as a criminal, by menacing and threatening victims.

Being a 'detective' and finding work for the divorce courts was easy. Jesse Farbrother in Brighton (the place most celebrated for adultery evidence scenes) opened an account at Barclay's Bank under the name of The Gibbons Bureau. A client called Manning, just seventeen, then saw an advertisement in the local paper asking for 'a young lady with detective abilities.' Farbrother met his new recruit and said that he had a big staff of 'eighteen permanent and twenty on reserve.' He detailed young Manning to follow a man from Brighton to London on five journeys, and also to watch a woman's flat. The whole business became farcical in court when the judge and jury learned that Farbrother had wandered the land trying to open detective agencies. Farbrother had even created a detective companion kit to be given to each agent, including a tab that had to be dropped on the ground if ever they were lost while on an assignment.

Crazy stories of 'detectives' proliferated as the popular media made them glamorous. Magazines such as *Union Jack* and the *Sexton Blake Library* (the latter started in 1915) had led to such innovations as 'The Dog Detective' and the blurb typified the appeal of the detective for readers: 'A Sexton Blake story means something really first class in the way of detective fiction. And you can get one every week! Stories that get you worked up with excitement, stories in which baffling mystery, non-stop action, brilliant detection and thrills are welded into one masterly whole … ' Such was the impact, that tales like that of the 'sham detective' William Martin who was arrested for theft of thirty-two sides of bacon. He had carried out the theft by approaching a young boy who was in charge of the van-load of bacon, saying he was a detective and showing a badge. The boy said, 'I have seen detectives on the films wearing badges, so I believed him.'

Both private detectives on divorce cases and Scotland Yard men involved in special duties were bringing to light a whole tranche of new issues related to the morality of detective work. A detective had to encroach on personal liberties in the course of his or her work; investigative actions would sometimes border on crossing the line into criminality, at least as far as the letter of the law would define in a criminal law court. This whole area of detective work became apparent during the Great War when 'spy mania' meant that Vernon Kell and his new MI5 were intercepting letters; Kell, as we have noted, worked with the Yard, and Yard men would learn to act as agents, with a more military purpose.

These difficulties became more widely understood with the Janvier case of 1917, which went to the Court of Appeal in 1919. Henriette Janvier had come from Paris to London in 1908 to learn English, sent there by her employers. In London she met a German called Neumann. But the problem with this case was that the detectives in question were described as 'private enquiry agents.' They were almost certainly working for the Yard and for Kell. What happened was that when the lodging house was almost empty one day in 1917, the agents arrived and told Henriette that another lodger called March was corresponding with a spy, but on his first appearance, one of the agents had said, 'I am a Detective Inspector from Scotland Yard and represent the military authorities, and you are the woman we want, as you have been corresponding with a German spy.'

There had clearly been a change of tactics since the original trial, in which no sentences had been given. The truth was either that the two men really were Yard officers doing the usual thing of intercepting suspect mail, or they were indeed private agents. If the latter is true, then they would have had no palpable reason for being on such a detail and to act as aggressively as they did. The incident illustrates the extent to which the presence of a Scotland Yard detective instilled awe and fear into private citizens. Of course, the affair with Henriette was in war time, but in effect the detectives were asking the girl to co-operate in an enquiry – one that breached civil rights – without prior arrangement. Moreover, they did so after terrifying her first.

The other mainline development in the years up to the post-Second World War years was the refinement of records. This incorporates the Criminal Records Office, which developed from the Habitual Criminals Register and has existed since 1871, together with the General Registry, within the Records Management Branch (QPP3). Records from Special Branch were separated from the main stock in 1946. The General Registry covers virtually everything from accidents to transport; two indices are maintained in addition, the Names Index and Tag Index. The second one deals with matters by subject areas.

Writing in 1953, the crime correspondent of *The Daily Telegraph*, Stanley Firmin, gave a brilliant description of records at a time when the outstanding detective Robert Lee was working in the CRO. Firmin writes:

> Housed in the Criminal Records Office is the world's most complete collection of facts about individual criminals. That collection, built up over long years, consists of much more than many hundreds of thousands of finger-prints. It has long embraced in addition the filing away of all kinds of personal data about individual men and women crooks throughout Britain.

Lee went to work in Records, and his work there illustrates the benefits of persistent use of information and sifting of data; Firmin explained that Lee built up a mind's eye picture of the person, from the details on squares of cardboard. He also came up with new ways of filing the records. His thesis for the innovations was that detailed knowledge constructed a personal profile, and that in turn became something that could be extended into predictive thinking – anticipating crimes. The evidence for this is in a case in which Lee and Records teamed up with the Ghost Squad, a special cadre of men and women which lasted from 1945 to 1949, devised as a network of officers within ordinary disguise, taking on close observation of suspects. It was a concept familiar to espionage masters, of course. It was conceived by Percy Worth and developed by Commissioner Sir Ronald Howe. There is no doubt that the Squad was effective: in those few years their activities brought about 769 arrests and the recovery of over £200,000 worth of goods.

There is some doubt, but it does appear that Ghost Squad members were sometimes bribed and corrupted, and this happened in Lee's famous case, the dogged pursuit of a gang of robbers led by C.S. William Chapman of the Flying Squad (nicknamed The Terrier because of his determined and patient pursuit of suspects). Lee studied a long list of burglaries and looked for a pattern; he found one. The line of thought came from a broken key in a safe, which turned out to be a unique key made by just one firm. Chapman then set about using the Ghost Squad to watch every employee, as it seemed certain that an employee was part of the burglary ring. The observations lasted a very long time and there was a breakthrough, but in spite of Lee's excellent work, there appears to have been some corruption of officers. In the end, the spy in the Yard was outwitted by Lee, who devised the clever method of placing false duty rotas in the books, so the spy could not have accurate information to pass on to the crooks. The spy was never found, but the mastermind of the criminals, Santro the safe-breaker, was eventually caught, along with most (but not all) of the gang.

By the end of the Second World War then, detectives in all areas of life were proliferating, but Scotland Yard itself and the CID were emerging into a massive, many-sided organisation, with ever-increasing numbers of specialists and departments.

9

MAJOR CASES c.1900-40

An overview of the careers of the detectives that figured in important cases as the Yard moved into action on increasingly challenging serious crime, highlights the character and abilities of the officers better than statistics. In other words, we judge and understand these officers by their involvement in the cases that presented them with opportunities to use their talents. But there are other things to be learned about how and why Britain came to have the highly respected detective force that it now has. What also emerges from the chronicles of serious crime is how the people who took on those roles saw themselves.

Primarily, much of the interest lies in that aspect of detective work that is rooted in the person beneath the public image and the duties concerned. Some celebrated detectives were lucky; others relied on established traditional methods; some tried to make their profession closer to the novels and films than to reality. Many, as we will see in the last chapter, courted celebrity and drama or even controversy. As the new professionals moved from those chasing Jack the Ripper with very little forensic or sophisticated organisational back-up, to officers with an armoury of science and logistics behind them, they transmuted into much more than embodiments of a military cast of mind. They actually came to be impressively skilled at adapting to changing crime and criminals, and reading through the notoriously difficult and complex murders for instance, it is easy to see this process in action. The following case studies are looked at more for what detectives did than for the narrative of the crimes themselves.

The Moat Farm Murder, 1903

The facts are simple, but the story and the people's actions were not, when Moat Farm is considered. The tale is of the disappearance of Camille Holland, who went missing from her home at Moat House Farm in Essex. She was wealthy: so much so that she bought the farm herself and then set up home with one Samuel Dougal. It seems hard to understand how this happened, given the fact that Dougal had been incarcerated in an asylum, and had also had three previous marriages. Camille went missing in June 1899, but Dougal was spending her money and he ran away before the police could come too close and ask awkward questions. But he was tracked down and shortly after that Camille's body was discovered in a ditch.

Ballistics evidence showed that Dougal was the killer, but there had been a lot of good work done by Inspector Eli Bower of the Yard. At the beginning of the search for Camille's body, Bower was sent down to Essex. He did the obvious thing first: searched the entire place from top to bottom. But the search met with no success. Bower was working with Sergeant Scott of Essex, and as they moved from inside to the moats and ditches, they went down to the mud. It was here that deduction came into play, enough to make Sherlock Holmes proud. Scott surmised that the reason the body had not been found could be because it had been weighted, so that it would sink through the water and into the mud.

That was the theory, but there were plenty of ditches and it was taking a very long time to search them all. Bower busied himself finding out about Dougal's activities on the farm, asking anyone who might have known or seen him. The first step towards the breakthrough was when he learned that there was a ditch that had been completely filled in – but that had been done before Dougal and Camille arrived. Only the men who had filled it in would have been able to locate it, so Bower began a search for them. It was a case of scouring the country for miles around, questioning all labouring men, and it paid off. A character known as 'Old Pilgrim' was the one who had done the work and he was brought in. The body was found and was proved to be that of Camille Holland.

Despite a series of elaborate statements from Dougal to the effect that the killing had been accidental, he was found guilty of murder, and was executed on 8 July 1903. His guilt and charging was entirely down to Bower and Scott's deductive work and, more than anything else, sheer dogged searching and questioning.

Dr Crippen and Walter Dew, 1910

Crippen, an American with interests in fringe medicine and dentistry, settled with his wife, musical artiste Belle Elmore, in North London in 1900. Their address has become one of the most notorious in the history of murder: 39, Hilldrop Crescent. They had a strange, unconventional life; Belle was a member of the music hall and variety fraternity but had very little work; she took in paying guests to make ends meet. Crippen became very friendly with a secretary, Ethel Le Neve, and after spending time together with little thought for what people might think it became obvious to many in their circle that Belle was not at home – or anywhere else. Crippen concocted a fabrication that she had returned to America because her mother had died, and then later he broke the news that Belle herself was dead. But eventually her worried friends, with plenty of cause for suspicion, went to tell the police about Belle's disappearance.

The man who took charge of the investigation was Walter Dew. He was from Northamptonshire, and was forty-seven at that time; he had been in the Metropolitan Police for thirty years and had been part of the group of detectives working on the Jack the Ripper case. When the Crippen case came along, he came to realise the importance of it, and how it would engage the public imagination. He sat and listened to the story told by John Nash and Lil Hawthorne, two of Belle's closest friends, and then he went, together with Sergeant Arthur Mitchell, to pay a call on Crippen.

Belle had indeed been murdered; Crippen had shot her and buried her under the floor of the cellar. The Crippens had a French servant, and she opened the door to Dew. It was to be a visit that would cause recriminations aimed at Dew later on. Ethel Le Neve was in the house: a point that was of utmost significance of course. Crippen was at work at his business address and Dew insisted that Ethel went with them to that address. Dew's words when he came face to face with Crippen are loaded with irony to this day:

> I am Inspector Dew and this is Sergeant Mitchell, of Scotland Yard. Some of your wife's friends have been to us concerning the stories you have told them about her death, with which they are not satisfied. I have made exhaustive enquiries and I am not satisfied so I have come here to see you to ask if you care to offer any explanation.

Dew was a very experienced policeman. He was being careful; so cautious was he that he began to take a very long statement and soon the two men were delving deeply into Crippen's life. It was then that a truly unusual step was taken – the detective and Crippen had lunch together. As they sat in an Italian restaurant in Holborn, naturally Dew was studying his suspect. But Crippen ate heartily and appeared to be free from any nervous anxieties or defensive manoeuvres in the conversation. All of which encouraged Dew to take an open-minded view of matters.

It was late in the afternoon before attention switched to Ethel. Her story, told repeatedly after the terrible events of the murder and the aftermath, was that she was deceived by Crippen. Dew had come up against a criminal capable of misleading anyone, as he presented to the world an eccentric mix of professionalism and bluster. But when Crippen and Ethel were on the run to Holland with the intention of travelling from there to America, Dew went with his sergeant back to Hilldrop Crescent and it was then that the discovery of Belle's body was made. This time, the search was a thorough one; first they found a pistol in a cupboard and a sheet of paper with Belle's signature written on it.

After that it was only a matter of time before they reached the cellar and on 13 July 1910, Dew tested the bricks on the floor with a poker, when the end of it slipped between two bricks. It was then a case of going down there. Dew wrote later, 'Presently a little thrill went through me … I then produced a spade from the garden and dug the clay that was immediately beneath the bricks. After digging down to a depth of about four spadefuls I came across what appeared to be human remains.' It was big business for the Yard. The Assistant Commissioner came to the scene: MacNaghten, who had the presence of mind to take cigars with him to help cope with the noxious fumes that Dew had said were emanating from the remains.

One remarkable aspect of this dig in the cellar was the way in which the scene of crime was not 'safe' in terms of forensic methodology. Disinfectant was used, for instance, and therefore all kinds of substances had been removed which may well have been important later. Of course the hunt for the fugitives was then in process.

In the annals of detection, the Crippen case is, of course, celebrated as being the first time that the telegraph was used to help capture a murderer. But the 'detective work' was actually done by the commander of the ship that Crippen and Ethel were on, the *Montrose*. This was Henry Kendall, and he was very observant. Ethel was travelling in the clothes of a young man, and for most of the time this seems to have been effective; but Kendall had slight suspicions when he saw the clothes and noted that her movements were not masculine. Finally, he saw Ethel squeezing Crippen's hand and it was this detail that led to his certainty that here he had the fugitives on his ship.

The wireless telegraph was then used, somewhat momentously; the submarine cable had been used sixteen years earlier to catch a murderer called Muller who was also on board ship heading for America. Another killer, named Tawell, had been spotted on a train and the telegraph was used to make sure that police were waiting for him as he alighted. The wireless telegraph was used now and a dramatic pursuit on a faster ship meant that Dew was waiting for Crippen when he docked.

The elements of the case are well-known, but the most interesting aspect of the arrest and the following events are in the relationship of the media with the detectives involved. Dew made enemies, as he did not co-operate. Naturally, he was the subject of a media frenzy and was offered large amounts of money for his story. So high profile was the case that, as the build-up to the trial proceeded, the Pinkerton agency were brought in, their task being to protect key witnesses who had to journey over the Atlantic to London. Criticisms of Dew's handling of the whole affair, right from the start, now began. Even the famous judge, Sir Travers Humphreys, joined in with the criticism, such as the fact that Belle's furs were still at Hilldrop Crescent – an oversight on Dew's part at the time of his first inspection there. The essence of that line of thought was the rhetorical question: what woman would go to America for a lengthy stay and not take her furs?

Buck Ruxton, 1935

On the quiet road across the borders from Dumfries, travellers saw the remains of a human arm below a bridge and from that initial discovery a series of events led to forensic work that was destined to revolutionise the science and to add something to the art and science of detection that would lead to massive advances in its technique.

Dr Buck Ruxton, whose practice was in Lancaster, was not exactly smart when he cut up his wife and maid. He wrapped some remains in a local newspaper. Detective Inspector Hayward of the Yard went north to visit the editor of *The Sunday Graphic*. The newspaper recovered with the body turned out to be one of a limited print-run; police were then sent to each of the nineteen newsagents that had deliveries of that edition. Of course, as two women had been reported missing in Lancaster, the Lancaster newsagent (who actually took the largest number of copies) was spoken to.

Ruxton (real name Buckhtyar Hakim from Bombay) was very jealous and his wife Isabella was, in his mind at least, a problem: he considered her to be unfaithful and moreover the poor woman had even tried to kill herself at one point. Ruxton was indeed very careless as clothing that was found also helped to have him traced in connection with the body parts. The crucially important factor in this famous case is the fact that Mrs Ruxton had protruding front teeth and features of her skull, and that of Rogerson, were studied alongside photographs of the women. The photographs were enlarged so that they compared in size to the reconstructed skulls found in the papers; when these were both traced onto paper the contours matched. Negative images brought out the protruding teeth very clearly, from the shape in the photographs and also from the bones themselves.

Such work with superimposed pictures had not been done previously; but there was still more to come, this time in the specialised world of microbiology. A professor with knowledge of the variety of maggot called *calliphora* went to work on the creatures' life cycle and so could, with their presence in the bones and flesh, calculate the time of death.

Ruxton, who also proved to be a bigamist, was hanged at Strangeways in May 1936. So deeply did the Ruxton case enter popular culture that there a song was written on it, to the rhythm of 'Red sails in the Sunset', with these words:

Red stains on the carpet,
Red stains on your knife,
Oh, Dr Buck Ruxton, you cut up your wife;
The nursemaid she saw you, and threatened to tell –
So, Dr Buck Ruxton, you killed her as well.

The Dobkins Case, 1941

The Second World War London Blitz was mayhem in all kinds of ways, mainly concerning massive damage to property and large loss of life from the bombing raids. But that new and horrific landscape of desolation also provided opportunities for crooks. In fact, for one man it was a convenient situation in which to murder his wife and make sure that her body was hidden in the ruins. But his plans did not quite work out and what emerged from the case was a landmark in the use of dental records in detective work.

Harry Dobkins was a firewatcher in Kensington and his wife, Rachel, disappeared not long after a bombing on a chapel. Their relationship had been stormy to say the least. Rachel had threatened suicide on several occasions. They separated and Dobkins was not only remiss with payments to her, but he was in the habit of being handy with his fists when she was around as well. When she went missing, police were naturally suspicious. Her sister went to a police station and stated that she thought there might have been 'foul play' involved in Rachel's disappearance. Detectives went to search the chapel. But her handbag had been found elsewhere, so there was always the possibility that she had wandered off somewhere else, maybe a long distance away, such was her unstable mental condition. But then a clearance worker, close to the area of the chapel where the detectives had been, found something.

He found Rachel's body – or at least a bunch of mangled remains. The renowned pathologist, Keith Simpson, studied the remains and felt that the death could have been caused by a bomb because the limbs had been blasted off and scattered. But Simpson was thorough and persistent and he then saw that in fact the head had been cut from the trunk. Detectives felt that this may have been the missing Mrs Dobkins, but they had to find a way to be sure about that.

Teeth had been known to be unique to the person since the early years of the twentieth century; a burglary involving teeth-marks in cheese had led to the conviction of a man at that time. There had also been a case of murder on the continent in which teeth identification had been used. Now this was applied to the Dobkins corpse. Very conveniently, her dentist had kept good records and he had a profile of her teeth and notes on what fillings she had had in which teeth. Specific fillings in molars did the trick of identifying Mrs Dobkins. Even specific nerve-roots matched the records of work done on her mouth. Harry Dobkins was charged and sentenced to hang.

Keith Simpson's work on the Dobkins case and on the remains of Mrs Dobkins entailed the use of his own photographic methods. Gradually, throughout the 1930s, forensic science was being refined into something with increasing degrees of accuracy in a study of a whole range of human physiology.

Thompson and Bywaters, 1922

The young detective David Nixon ('Nixon of the River') spent some time guarding the young Fred Bywaters and had no idea at the time that he was playing a small part in that grand narrative of death and passion. The case centred on the triangle of Percy Thompson and his wife Edith, together with her lover, Bywaters. The importance of this case, in which P&O writer Bywaters developed a passionate relationship with Edith, is that it led to Bywaters fatally stabbing Mr Thompson one night, and what emerged was that variety of murder narrative in which there is both fantasy and romance, yet mixed in such a way that two people can conspire to kill in order to be together. What young Nixon concluded brings out the importance of this kind of subject for detective study of character and motivation. He realised that he had enjoyed an ordinary conversation with a bright and perky young man, no more than that.

When his superior, Detective Wensley, explained who the man was, Nixon still considered that there was a certain kinship between them and that murder was something extraneous to that. As Nixon had seen, it was a learning curve about criminal psychology: the case highlighted the complexity of murderous motives.

Stanley Setty

The notion of a murder as something linked to a need for two people to be together to the exclusion of everyone else, even turning to murder in order to do so, was nothing at all to do with the kind of killings that emerged during and after the Second World War. It was, in many ways, the arrival of the psychopathic killer. As far as Scotland Yard were concerned (and the regional detectives too) these people presented something entirely new. The figures of Haigh, Christie and Heath stand out in this respect, but the story of Stanley Setty is not so well-known, though he too represented this new type of criminal.

The fascination of the case is that Setty was killed and taken out to sea, then dropped, in the belief that the body would never be found. Setty was really Sulman Seti, born in Baghdad, but when his family came to England, he gradually became a self-made businessman and was known in London as a pavement dealer: he cashed cheques on commission – large amounts of the latter. He operated in the cheaper pubs and clubs around Marble Arch and was known to the law. But he made enemies and caused jealousies. He went missing before an arranged meeting about the sale of a Wolseley saloon. He disappeared in September and by late October there was no evidence that anything foul had happened to him, but his family offered a large reward for knowledge of where Stanley might be.

At that point the detectives moved in and began their work, because a body was found in the Essex marshes; it was a bundle of severed limbs and a torso. In came the experts from the Yard, including the great fingerprint man Cherrill. It was one of his finest moments, because he had to take away some of the wrinkled skin and then stretch it on his own fingers to re-align the configurements of the person's prints. Setty had a record and so the identity of the corpse was traced.

People who had been with Setty and had monetary transactions were soon found because he used five pound notes and at that time all these notes were tagged in use, due to rarity. The detectives found a man called Donald Hume, and there was the psychopathic type par excellence. Hume lived, as Neville Heath did, a life of fantasy, performance and roles enmeshed in excitement and risk. He had served in the RAF and then started a life sustained by a series of frauds. He had rowed with Setty and in a fight Hume took a dagger and stabbed his enemy to death. Hume used his pilot skills to fly the body out to sea, thinking that would be the last of him. How wrong he was.

But Hume was the 'Scarlet Pimpernel' of crime; he shifted locations and identity with alacrity and could put on a convincing performance under intense interviewing if he needed to. He was tried twice and acquitted both times on murder charges; Hume's murder of Setty was given a fantastic narrative by him, embellished by supposed contact with three gangsters who had threatened him and allegedly killed Setty. As no prints were found in the flat where the police were certain that he had killed Setty, then nothing could be certain in the prosecution at the trial. He was released and eventually moved to Europe where he assumed another name – John Stanislav, an American this time. But this time, in Switzerland, he was charged and convicted of a robbery and murder. He was given a life sentence. But regarding the Setty killing, Hume sold his confession to a newspaper: 'I Killed Setty and Got Away With Murder' the story ran.

When Hume was sent back to England in 1976 he was given a psychiatric examination and transferred to Broadmoor. In the history of detectives and detection in Britain he represents that dangerous homicidal fabulist whose pursuit and interrogation stretched all the resources of technology and intellect available at the time in the Yard. The fact that his antics saved him from the murder conviction (and the noose) was a typology of things to come. Detectives would increasingly be called upon to cope with adversaries who tended to enhance criminal proclivities with whatever offered them opportunities in the latest technology, business organisation or 'domino effect' from other sources in the greater macro-economic factors above and beyond local crime. Of course, in London, these factors would be all the more immediate and accessible.

Of course, inextricably bound up with all this was gangland, and that had always been the major opposition for the detective forces, since 'Jim the Penman' in mid-Victorian times. In 1948 one particular event epitomises what organisational logistics were forced upon the Yard and the regional counterpart: this was the so-called battle of Heathrow. The gangland leader Jack Spot was always given the credit of being the mastermind behind this attempted robbery of bullion at the partially constructed Heathrow. The plan was to arrive in numbers at a bonded warehouse, in the night, well armed of course, and to take the gold from a plane due to arrive from South Africa.

What happened was that, despite several planning sessions and a great deal of thought on the part of the villains, and having a man employed by BOAC who was essential to the job, it went wrong. The fact was that there was an informer as well: this led to what became known as Operation Nora by the Yard; as the 'plant' from the gang was to take knock-out drops for the guards to take, the detective group chose some men to play the part of those guards; they would pretend to be out cold when the crooks arrived.

Operation Nora was planned with back-up and good positions, or so it seemed. Flying Squad men joined regular detectives and by 11 p.m. that night there were no less than fourteen officers there, with reserves hidden not far away, behind some cases. The officers, under Superintendent Bob Lee, wore BOAC uniforms and carried on as if all was normal. The unfortunate officers who offered to be 'drugged' were in for a hard time; the gang arrived and one of the detectives was clouted on the head with an iron bar just to make sure he was out cold. The crooks were armed with bars, coshes and even garden shears. All hell broke out then, when DI Roberts shouted out, 'We are police officers of the Flying Squad! Stand where you are!' The villains did nothing of the sort and a battle ensued.

Lee was badly wounded; the shears did devastating work on some officers, and it was only because there were reserves outside who finally came to resolve things, that there was not more severe injury and perhaps even loss of life. As historian Donald Thomas has written, this 'battle' was seen as a real triumph for the Yard: 'It was the most dramatic battle in the history of the Flying Squad and was widely seen as a major victory at last in the struggle against post-war crime.' There was also a final irony, in that the aircraft carrying the targeted bullion never arrived, being delayed by fog.

On all the major fronts of criminality then, the developments in detective work in the inter-war years and in the years immediately after the war gradually came to confront and handle matters very well. Some offensives against new versions of crime took a long time to mature and others, like the Ghost Squad, were abandoned. But the central initiatives such as the Flying Squad, the Records and the forensic sections, had all equipped themselves well in that time. There were undoubtedly some charismatic men and women in the ranks in that period also; it was a period in which detective work was flowering and changing in all kinds of contexts. For instance, Ada Atherton became the first female detective in the Transport Police when she began work at Waterloo in May 1924.

There were also reforms on a grand scale under Lord Trenchard. He was a man with an impressive military record who was pressed into service to sort out organisation and training, being appointed Commissioner in 1931. One of the persistent problems he was expected to put right was the ongoing statistic that gave depressingly low figures of arrests due mainly to the speed of stolen cars in the crooks' escapes. Trenchard did the usual things: introduced economies and took measures that today would be called 'rationalising'. What was due to happen was that training and recruitment were to be revolutionised and streamlined; since a Committee on Police Powers and procedure of 1929 made a positive report recommending selection of senior officers with more rigour, changes were coming. Trenchard seemed like the man for that job: he and others around him wanted to recruit men with a high level of traditional education.

Training of detectives was due to be an important part of all this and a Police College was discussed. In the next chapter attention turns to the issue of the training of detectives and to the matter of a short-service system – another of Trenchard's ideas.

10

THE MAKING OF YARD MEN

Trenchard was Commissioner for just five years; he was an air-marshall who had served in the Boer War and in Ireland. He had been Commander of the Royal Flying Corps in the Great War and then played a major role in the creation of the RAF itself. His regime in the police brought about many radical changes, including bringing in a Statistical department and a Daily Crime Telegram; he created a Detective Training School and a Police Scientific Laboratory. The Training School at Hendon was his work too. In more difficult areas he was arguably reticent, as in the known activities which were undoubtedly corrupt. He also challenged the policy, going back to the beginnings with Peel, of promoting from within. Trenchard saw the virtues of a short-service scheme.

What Trenchard did was to make the Police College the place where the real 'career men' would be trained and encouraged to use their talents, and to offer finite career periods to others. A short-term contract would allow a recruit to sign on for just ten years before retiring with a gratuity payment. His short-lived regime was assured some kind of continuance, however, as he appointed Sir Philip Game to succeed him – a man who could be relied on to act as if he were still an aide-de-camp.

The world's first training programme for detective work began in 1936 on the Hendon Police College Estate. By the Metropolitan Police Act of 1933, Hendon was established as the centre for police training. It was opened in 1934 and was clearly an institution that became indispensable as it was renewed after the Second World War.

We have memoirs about how men became detectives and these help us to understand what the motivations were. The middle line in this was discontentment with the beat work of the 'ordinary copper'. Leonard Nipper Read, for instance, 'the man who caught the Krays', explains it in that way, and that the course at Hendon Police College, which he attended in 1947, was 'Drilling and lectures on public order, diseases of animals, child neglect, company fraud, incest, rape, bigamy, sodomy, helping children at school crossings, suicide, infanticide, drunks, ponces and traffic control.' Read started as a detective when a senior officer said he had a job for him and that he would be working in plain clothes.

Before the new training, though, a bright policeman – or a restless one – followed a set procedure of application to become a detective as explained in a biography of Nixon, later Detective Inspector;: the method was outlined by a senior officer:

> He outlined the routine. An applicant wrote his name in the book pro-
> vided for the purpose in the Station. In due course, as vacancies occurred,
> if he were considered by the Station Detective Sergeant as a possibility his
> name was forwarded through the usual channels and he was interviewed
> by the Divisional Detective Inspector. If the interview was satisfactory
> the applicant was posted for CID duties as an 'aide' when he was tried
> out on his own …

Read was a man who went through that process twenty years later, and he explained that as an aide you have a mentor. He began at St John's Wood and there his mentor was Martin Walsh, of whom Read wrote: 'I was put under the wing of one of the best detectives I have ever met … He was an older man, in his forties, who was used as a 'tutor' aide. He taught me what investigating was all about.' In that way, Nixon and Read learned to be detectives by working on the streets with experienced men. But what about the new men going to the college?

A great deal can be learned about that curriculum from the 1938 *Report of the Departmental Committee on Detective Work and Procedure.* This report outlines the whole course of training, from a review of general detective work, through to specific skills such as crime record-keeping and photography. The document was produced by a team led by Sir Samuel Hoare, Secretary of State for the Home Office. In terms of commentary on existing detective work, the report puts considerable emphasis on communication between individual officers and indeed at the group operational level, as in comments about detectives from different forces gathering to exchange information at race meetings. Men asked in the course of the enquiry had repeatedly suggested that detective work would be notably improved if a 'spirit of co-operation was fostered.'

The 1930s was the time at which it was properly registered that liaison across the country was becoming crucially important in police work. The report recommended bringing senior officers from different forces together so that they could work together at the earliest opportunity in the process of investigating a specific crime. The normal practice at the time, if a man had to go to work in another area, was for the officer to notify the CID concerned, though the report's authors noted a very uneven application of this principle. They advised individual procedures, but stressed that an effective system of intelligence about criminals was at the top of the list of requirements. In the years immediately before the 1938 report, 'lending' of officers had been very small scale, and it is clear that these instances were for particular expertise; just twenty lendings took place in the years between 1931 and 1936. Naturally, in murder cases, this kind of lending activity is more important, and the authors reported that the recent results were encouraging:

> In the five years 1931-35 there were known to the police 460 cases of murder or suspected murder of persons aged one year or over [others were infanticide since 1922]. In 181 of these cases the murderer ... committed suicide, leaving 279 cases to be detected ... arrests were made in 254 cases ...

Training of officers received close attention. After all, numbers of offic-. ers were accelerating quickly and the force was huge compared to the men at work in the Ripper years five decades before this. In 1938 there were 1,198 CID personnel; Liverpool and Birmingham had equivalent forces of over a hundred men. As recruitment was clearly increasing, it was a good time to take stock of needs and of methods. All the obvious issues were discussed in the course of exploring the nature of the detective needed in that time of inter-war expansion of organised crime, rackets and robberies. One of the central points considered was the idea of a probationary period, the line of thought parallel to the 'aide' system. The panel concluded that no probation was needed but conceded that a detective is 'always on probation' in that he or she must always be 'subject to continuing to discharge duties successfully … '

The syllabus for training recommended in the report was based on the question of integration or separation from the normal police training syllabus. The decision made was that a thirteen-week course was necessary for detective recruits. In addition to that recruits were to spend six weeks attached to a CID as in the aide system. In terms of the content of the syllabus, this is, in summary form, the course decided on:

Week 1   Conduct and professionalism; dealing with the press; prevention of crime; co-operative detective work; use of scientific aids; intelligence reports; local knowledge; observation and special contexts for work.

Week 2   Finger Prints; Judges' Rules; telephone and wireless; use of cars; photography; searching scene of crime.

Week 3   Legal knowledge – summonses; warrants; powers of arrest; identification parades; prisoners' rights; larceny; receivers; housebreaking notation and study of scene; robbery.

Week 4   Sexual offences; knowledge of obscene publications; infanticide.

Week 5   Homicide law; scene of crime photography; coroners and inquests; wounds; blood groups; poisoning; explosives offences; arson; financial fraud and fraud in use of materials.

Week 6   Bribery and corruption; blackmail; Official Secrets Acts; pro-
            cedure in courts; reports to other forces.
Week 7   Dangerous drugs; courts; extradition.
Week 8   Depositions; dying declarations; testimony of the sick.

This is, as would be expected, very thorough and wide-ranging. Police work expands and becomes more complex as the population increases and the knock-on effects of industrial and urban growth continue. At the time of the report, all manner of recent developments were absorbed into the thinking behind that syllabus. To take one example: the first Official Secrets Act was passed in 1911 but there had been a second one in 1920, and a third was in preparation as this report was written, to become statute law the next year, 1939. A detective would have to become acquainted with such topics as knowing which places were prohibited and why, and to whom; how communication of classified information could or would be passed; and how to access accommodation addresses of suspects. Another example of the complexity and also the delicacy of the knowledge absorbed is the awareness of the 'dying declaration'. It was not uncommon, in an age well before motorways, for a police officer to find him or herself in an ambulance on the way to hospital with a dying victim of a murderous attack. The dying declaration would be crucially important and would need to be written carefully verbatim. In one case, an old man had been beaten almost to death by two assailants in a lonely farmhouse; he spoke in the ambulance to the police officer about the attackers' accents, saying they sounded Chinese. That detail led to a string of events in the ensuing investigation.

One very important topic approached by the report was the ongoing issue of records. There were, of course, ever-growing records in all counties and areas and the authors of the report saw the central importance of this being rationalised and unified in terms of method and control. It might have been stating the obvious, but the point was made that 'It is important that the functions of the Criminal Record Office should not be assumed by any regional record centre …' and that a

Main Fingerprint Index should be maintained. The Clearing House system would be maintained and reviewed, in order to make sure that the right information was directed to the right place.

What about the more people-centred aspects of the new detective work? One of the most enlightening examples of this is in the details about photography in the report. An appendix goes into specific detail about the procedure and knowledge that the detective using photography for records must have. There are technical drawings of all equipment and very particular images of the chair on its turntable. The basis of this work was the maintenance of the card index record. This had ten sections of information to be listed in the right places. After that, seven categories of index are described. If we add to this the expected knowledge of publications and the up-dating of basic criminological knowledge, then the work of the detective could easily become 'paperwork' so we have to ask about the supposed excitement and appeal of the profession at that time. The answers are in a study by Percy Hoskins, referred to previously. In his richly-illustrated guide to detective training as it was around 1955, Hoskins gives a clear idea of how that conception in the report of twenty years earlier had become a workable system. His book, *No Hiding Place*, is a feel-good advert for Scotland Yard while it also explains all the intricacies of the work for the layperson.

Hoskins' hypothetical detective recruit begins with his thirteen weeks at Peel House, the new venue after the Second World War. He then becomes a detective recruit for a year, and then to Hendon. The basis is practical all the way: 'The paramount need for keen observation is again drilled into the men's heads. The theory of the Yard is that a good description is better than any picture and its detectives are taught to cultivate retentive memories as a matter of routine.' Then the recruit is faced with the more academic side of work – criminal law, for instance. The practice then was for both senior detectives and lawyers to work on the prosecution.

Hoskins interviewed Commander Rawlings, Deputy of the CID about detective work and the reply was, 'It is 95% perspiration, 3% inspiration and 2% luck!' On top of all the good advice and legal material, the college was equipped with as many kinds of device for simulation of events as possible, and every aid for information processing. These were such items as subject maps, study of facial characteristics, observation tests, use of scale models, anatomy; basic ballistics and forgery methods.

Of course, good training for work like this, with people involved all the way, has to have simulations. The training then entailed hypothetical cases and these were often printed in the *Police Review* which had been published since 1893, the intention being that all officers could and should constantly update their skills and keep sharp. A typical simulation would be in these stages:

> The discovery of a body. A tyre-mark is close to it.
>
> Recruit uses two-way radio for assistance and takes measurements.
>
> The body is then examined for hair, stains etc.
>
> Photography is then used for things such as tyre marks.
>
> Witnesses are interviewed.
>
> Enquiries made in adjacent buildings.
>
> Clues are then taken to the laboratory.
>
> As the forensics take place, the trainee traces owner of the car.
>
> The owner is selected at an identity parade.

It all seems very simple, but in essence, that sequence of events inevitably draws in a number of specialists; it entails skills of verbal communication, and it calls for a sense of close observation and deduction from available knowledge.

As for the more modern concepts and elements of detective work, some of the principal ones were around in the 1950s but not in operation or even generally accepted. For instance, offender profiling was conceived by Dr James Brussel in 1956 after a bomb explosion in a cinema in Brooklyn. It was the work of a criminal dubbed 'The Mad Bomber'. Brussel had worked with the CIA and the FBI on profiling in the war and he then studied case notes and went to work on the profile.

The doctor listed ten important features of the criminal, including the note that the man had 'an Oedipus complex'. Sure enough, a man was tracked down after a phone call.

But for more practical, people-centred detective skills, one of the most criticised elements of training has been interviewing technique. This situation has been exacerbated by prominent murder cases in which suspects who have emerged as mentally ill or with learning deficiencies have produced 'confessions' after interviewing. One remarkable case was in 1946, when two Scotland Yard detectives came north to the Lincolnshire area and interviewed a man who was a murder suspect. His housekeeper had been battered to death and investigation had opened up no other potential suspects. He was mentally at the age of fifteen, yet a quite sophisticated confession (in linguistic terms) was produced. But for a talented and strong-willed barrister, the man would quite probably have been hanged.

Training began in some old huts in Hendon; by 1973 Hendon was used again after a spell at Peel House in Knightsbridge. Obviously, training today has a high level of technology involved; but a report published in *Police Review* in June 2006 indicates that the CID is no longer seen as a glamorous job and new strategies are being used to attract recruits. Certainly, back in 1936 there was an appeal of glamour; but Hoskins' work relies heavily on the appeal of some of the features that had made life in the services appealing to many in the war such as advanced communications, fast cars, efficient fire-power, physical confrontation, and of course, a sense of a moral crusade against the 'forces of evil and anarchy' as put forward by magazines and comics.

Since the 1920s, the detective had been a figure in print and in illustration stemming from real operators such as Allan Pinkerton, the man who had worked in America. But there had also been the gangsterdom and organised crime in America during prohibition and the 'private dick' of the black and white crime films, and the new talkies, which had had an impact in Britain. The fictional private detectives Sam Spade and Philip Marlowe were there in celluloid and in print, but so also were the Yard men. The Flying Squad had made a detective career not only glamorous but dramatic – just the thing in 1945 to attract the types who had had the thrills and travel across the world, only to come home to routine and 9 'til 5 work. At the time of the report into detective training, crime novels set in England were selling prolifically: Ngaio Marsh's Inspector Alleyn first appeared in *A Man Lay Dead* in 1934; Agatha Christie created Superintendent Battle in *The Secret of Chimneys* in 1925; and Leo Bruce's Sergeant Beef appeared in *A Case for Three Detectives* in 1936.

Establishing the detectives in the years *c.*1930 to 1960 meant constant revisions of method, habits, ways of working, and most of all, in the personnel – the types of men who came along at the right time to use their talents well. Logically, the next step was to take the CID more efficiently out of 'Smoke' and into the regions, and this is where we will meet Leonard Nipper Read again. The strictures in the 1930s about more efficient communication with the regional forces gradually attained more importance. The old cry of 'Send for Scotland Yard' became more and more common as crime turned more violent and ruthless in the burgeoning new towns and the troubled Victorian ones. That call had been going on in a sense even before there was a Scotland Yard – since 1834 when people from a village in Wiltshire asked for help from 'Bow Street'. A pattern was established, and it is almost mythic. First there is a murder or a high level robbery; then the local police do all the traditional things but are baffled. Clearly, the more sophisticated officers in London will help, so call them in. Even the amateurs in fiction were called out for local horrors, the pattern being, arguably, Sherlock Holmes going to Dartmoor to sort out the ravages caused by the Hound of the Baskervilles.

11

IN AND OUT OF THE SMOKE

If the focus is switched from London to the regions, detective work takes on a different colour. So far the attention has been placed on the initiatives, developments and reforms at the very centre: the internal organisation of detective forces, the recruitment and training of officers and the cases by which advances were made. In the years from c.1950 to the massive events of the mid-1960s, there is a long sequence of regional cases in which Scotland Yard men participated, and of course, local and regional detective officers played a major role. Rather than methodically following general developments, this chapter looks at what happened in murder cases in those years, and what kinds of impact the events of the Great Train Robbery, the corruption scandal and the arrival of the Regional Crime Squads had on detective work.

The Regional Crime Squads arrived in 1966. They were based on earlier organisations in Birmingham set up by Chief Constable Edward Dodd. The rationale of these squads was explained by the Home Office in a press release:

> Regional Crime Squads are mobile groups of experienced detectives operating across Force boundaries. ... The National Co-ordinator supervises the progress made by the Regional Crime Squads and acts as a focal point for the collection of experience and the development of new ideas. He exercises a co-ordinating function when squads

from more than one region are required to take part in a particular operation.

It is necessary now to trace the lines of development across the previous twenty years, to understand how that significant new step was taken. The starting point is a case study of a murder early in that period in which detectives from London came north.

On Whitsun Saturday of 1957, Detective Superintendent Herbert Hannam and Detective Sergeant Rowe, both of the Yard, were on their way north to Halifax. They had been called in by the chief constable of the town very soon after the body of Emily Pye was discovered, brutally murdered, in the house behind her grocer's shop on Gibbet Street. Emily, aged eighty, had been severely bludgeoned to death in what one officer described as 'a rain of blows to the head' by a ruthless killer.

The town end of Gibbet Street is today in the heart of the Asian population's community; there is a mosque quite near to the shop which still stands where Emily's was all those years ago. The streets around are crowded and busy. The thoroughfare of Gibbet Street leads down to the centre of the town and is always noisy. In 1957 it was not so busy, but it is easy to imagine what it was like then, as the red-brick terraces still stand behind the current establishment, and Back Rhodes Street, in which her home stood and where she was killed, is still there, unchanged.

It was a Saturday when she died. Police later found that the shop and the house had been locked from around 1.45 p.m. Her body was discovered by her relatives, Mr and Mrs Wilson of Northowram, who had come to invite Emily to spend some of the holiday with them. Doris Wilson was her niece. But they found the premises locked, and through a window Derek Wilson saw the old lady's body, covered with a rug.

The whole investigation was dramatic and high-profile. The forensic specialists came, including Professsor Tryhorn from the Science Laboratory in Harrogate. Crowds gathered to watch as officers stood around talking, or walked through enclosed alleys, before action was taken. It was a senseless murder, apparently committed for a small amount of money taken from the till. It became clear that another, more substantial amount of money was hidden on the premises and had not been found. Superintendent Hannam said he would not have been able to find it. It was possible then, that the murder was not done by anyone who knew her and police at the time thought that it may have been an opportunistic killing by a passing casual customer, perhaps *en route* to Lancashire.

It was unusual for such a high-ranking officer to be there. Hannam was very highly thought of (he will be discussed at length in the next chapter); he was a smart, dapper man, wearing a Homburg and a very expensive suit. A picture in the local *Halifax Courier* shows him almost posing for the camera, looking dignified and impressive. Then forty-seven, he had been a leading figure in many West End cases and had been on assignments abroad.

The affair reached almost mythic status in the area for some time, as the very name 'Emily Pye' as an unsolved murder committed perhaps by an unknown assailant resonated through the local community. The woman had been such a popular and warm-hearted person, and had lived alone for fifteen years, but before that had had a 'life-long companion' for thirty years – as long as she had owned the business. At one time when she had been ill and had closed the shop while she was in hospital, she had told her niece that she thought a lot of the customers and ran the shop more as a hobby than anything else. All the more horrible then, that such a kind and sociable woman should die in that way.

Considerable force was used to kill Emily; it had all the hallmarks of a violent robbery and was representative of a template killing across the country. In the early to mid-1950s there had been a stream of such attacks on lonely women living alone, often on commercial premises. The ultimate irony is that in her death, the plain, low-key figure of Emily Pye attracted a media frenzy and a host of law officers who became local celebrities overnight. Such detail was given about Herbert Hannam that readers of the local papers were told that he wore 'designer' clothes and the information was given that his son was highly educated. Hannam was interviewed almost as if he were a heroic figure from a *Boy's Own*; much was made of his involvement in monetary fraud in the USA. He was, undoubtedly, a remarkably interesting figure to find walking around a northern industrial town.

But nothing came of the enquiry and it remained unsolved until a death-bed confession given to Calderdale Police in 2006, but the full details of that have not been released. Hannam and Rowe had come north, been highly visible, attracted the media, and then returned home. But Scotland Yard forays north were not always as steady and regulated as that. In 1958 thirteen inn managers in the Carlisle area were accused of obtaining property by false pretences, and fifty summonses were issued. That was following a Yard operation lasting for several months, *The Times* reported: 'Investigations by Scotland Yard officers began last August. Officers have made many visits to the city and neighbouring areas and many employees of the State scheme have been interviewed [Carlisle and District State Management Scheme]. Last February it was announced that enquiries had been completed … ' For almost seven months a team of detectives had descended on the area and worked methodically towards the arrests.

These two cases show, in marked contrast, the types of operations undertaken by the Yard in the 1950s. The acceleration of gun crime between *c.*1950 and 1965 meant that the 'corner shop', post office and bookmaker scenarios were increasingly common in murder cases. Clearly, gangland and the activities of the Krays and Richardsons kept many staff fully occupied, but in terms of the implementation of that kind of cross-country liaison advocated in the 1938 report, the more everyday killings such as that of Emily Pye were becoming the substance of much Yard detective work.

Another side of this same issue is the case of local and regional CID personnel. They were most vulnerable, and several local cases reveal the high level of risks undertaken by these officers against the increasing use of firearms by villains. A typical case from that era was the shooting of Detective Inspector Duncan Fraser in Huddersfield in 1951. After police training in Harrogate he became a detective officer in 1946 and moved to work in Huddersfield. There had been a number of break-ins in the area in early 1951 and Fraser, who was then head of Huddersfield CID, placed a farmhouse at Kirkheaton under observation. Three detectives – Fraser, Jenkins and Butler – along with police constables were briefed about that surveillance, and a cordon was put in place at the farm.

At around two in the morning, voices and shots were heard and an officer ran to the source of the sound. He found Fraser lying dead, and P.C. Jagger mortally wounded. Officers had been placed all around the vicinity but clearly there were errors in the arrangements. Alfred Moore, a poultry farmer from nearby Cockley Hill, was charged and later sentenced to death.

Detectives across the land, in and out of the 'Smoke' were more intensely subject to gun attacks. In arguably the most infamous and well mediated killing in this context we have the case of Gunther Podola. A description of Podola had been issued and Detective Sergeant Raymond Purdy cornered the suspect in a phone kiosk in South Kensington. There Purdy was shot after a chase into a nearby block of flats. The heartening part of the case is that Podola, who had broken away at that instant, was soon traced and the papers reported the arrest in great detail, reassuring the public that armed men on the loose were soon collared: 'The police received information that the man they wished to see was at the Claremont House Hotel ... Some thirty officers surrounded the hotel and a few moved into room 15, where they found a man on the bed ... '

In spite of stories of heroism and notable triumphs, the detective force was due to endure one of its most severe trials – in every sense – in the 1950s. The word 'corruption' filled the newspapers, and the man entrusted with much of the investigations into police corruption was Herbert Hannam. He was known as 'The Count' and by some 'The Suit' for his sartorial elegance. But he was also a hard and uncompromising character. In 1955, the commissioner of the Metropolitan Police, Sir John Nott-Bower, was anxious to make a statement about the conclusions of Hannam's investigations into named officers. He stated that 'The investigation ... arose out of two petitions dated June 26 1955 and July 21, 1955, to the Secretary of State from a prisoner in Maidstone Prison called Joseph Grech.' Grech had alleged corruption in three detectives, amounting to a perversion of the course of justice. In December of that year, all were convicted, along with five others. Therefore eight officers in total had been given custodial sentences for perjury or corruption.

Hannam's long investigation had involved thirty interviews, and the Commissioner was anxious to dispel a rumour that Hannam was about to see the Home Secretary about this unsavoury business. Grech was in gaol for larceny and housebreaking at the time. A month before this, Hannam had stood in the witness box at the Old Bailey reporting on this case of fabricated evidence. The evidence had been about a key in a trial from 1954. When Hannam interviewed a solicitor, he is alleged to have said,

> Our key and lock was a clever think-up and he ought to have been acquitted on that ... Some do, that's the luck of the game. I could name several of my clients who are inside for crimes which they are innocent ... I say nothing, for they have done plenty they were never caught for.

It was petitions from prison that turned the enquiry towards the officers concerned. The trouble for the corrupt officers began when Grech, a Maltese ponce, was charged with housebreaking so it seemed that a duplicate key had been used. But from Maidstone prison, he stated that the detective concerned in the case, along with others, had come up with the duplicate key idea and had accepted payments. At the Old Bailey, the full story emerged. Inspector Charles Jacobs, widely respected and the recipient of honours, was implicated. It was after that that Hannam was given the brief to investigate the generic collection of establishments where such collusion might be instigated between villains and police: that would cover casinos, brothels, the work of prostitutes and so on.

On top of that, there were missing files, reported by a woman who had seen some official files in a flat; Robertson admitted negligence in that respect. For Hannam, it was a difficult time. As Leonard Read, who knew him, said, 'Bert conducted the enquiry with the thoroughness and diligence which he brought to all his cases. In doing this he did himself no favours and earned the contempt of some junior officers, but more tragically, the mistrust of some senior ones.' It was largely a case of sorting out the 'rotten apples' as far as the senior command was concerned. Hannam was certain to be unpopular in conducting the business.

Two years later, a group of detectives drove to Brighton to arrest Detective Sergeant Trevor Heath. This was to prove to be another high profile corruption case. Heath's property and home were searched and he was interrogated; following that, a detective and no less a person than the Chief Constable were also arrested. Witnesses spoke about the top officers taking bribes to keep previous convictions out of evidence, and the centre of interest was the Astor Club close to the West Pier and a bookmaking business run by Sammy Bellson. The origin of much of the scandal was in the career of Alan Roy Bennett, a career criminal who, on his release from gaol in 1949, had bought the Astor Club. The place was rough and violence frequent, along with all kinds of receiving and illegal transactions; the allegation was that detectives had turned a blind eye to these things and even took a share of money stolen in the crooks' activities.

When a detective arrived in the area and met a certain Inspector Moody in a pub, he was stunned at the amount of money being spent on drink, and it was here that the suspicions started. The two detectives at the heart of these nefarious events were imprisoned for five years. Naturally, this was extremely embarrassing for Scotland Yard and for regional CID. The two affairs made it essential that the Yard engage in a forceful damage limitation exercise and the subject of the police establishment's relationship with the press and media has a key moment there, when the notion of what we now call 'public image' and 'Public relations' suddenly shifted to the top of the agenda at several meetings.

The story of the regional crime squads began not long after those regretful events. In April 1963, the Royal Commission on the Police made the idea a priority. It was decided then, in the very early stages, that the management should be arranged around the control of the General Inspector of Constabulary and that four chief superintendents would supervise the routine work of the squads. The planning stage was concerned with the need to disseminate information and to streamline the use and availability of scientific knowledge and expertise when required at any location. The unit was to be housed in Horseferry House, working integrally with the Home Office; the squads of that nature that already existed, in Birmingham, Bristol, Newcastle and London, worked on the principle of drawing officers from various places to work as a team for a specific purpose. The Home Secretary told the press that he believed this new force would 'strengthen the police at a crucial point.' It must have seemed a very ambitious notion at the time, even claiming to be planning to use skills and methodology from foreign forces and from within the Commonwealth.

By October 1964, the theory had clarified into a well structured design. There was to be a network of nine squads, superimposed on existing forces, and detectives working with the new squads would suspend their routine duties. The manpower of the new squads totalled 600 officers; each of nine districts was to have its own headquarters and a district co-ordinating officer was to lead each squad. Logically, it was fully understood that by c.1960 criminal rings were opening up all areas of the country and so they had to be met with similarly organised and efficient police opposition.

The nine districts were to be put in place for a trial period of two years and then reviewed. In 1962, the Home Office Police Research and Planning Branch had set to work to create this new initiative and a ruling influence in their innovations were the statistics on the rate of detected crimes: in 1957 there had been 545,562 indictable crimes and 47.2% were detected, and then by 1963 of 978,076 such crimes, only 43.1% were detected. There was a clear realisation that something more than a steady evolution was needed if there was to be any substantial impact that would change this trend.

In November 1964, Commander J.C. Bliss was appointed as the national co-ordinator of the RCS. That did not make him head of the CID, but he had proved his ability in working to rationalise the functions of the new squads, and his base was to be at Scotland Yard. He had been trained at Hendon and began his career as a police constable in London, following that with experience as a pilot in the RAF.

He became a detective in the Metropolitan Police in 1951, and was succeeded by Leonard Nipper Read, who summed up the virtues of the organisation simply and with practical common sense:

> I became as passionate about the squads as John had been, and I was increasingly aware of the constraints under which they worked. In one of my first annual reports I pointed out the problems associated with cross-border crimes, and suggested from the outset that such crimes should become the responsibility of the squad.

Read certainly had a point in noting that the squads had that limitation; between 1956 and 1958 the Scottish serial killer, Peter Manuel, had killed most of his victims in Scotland, but he had also come south and murdered Newcastle taxi driver Sydney Dunn in December 1957. A murder team of four detectives led by DCS John Hall conducted the investigation very well in spite of difficulties, but, in looking at the larger picture of Manuel's depredations in Scotland, the police work on both sides of the border would undoubtedly have been more efficient had the RCS system been in place in the way that Read suggested.

It did not take long for the squads to prove that they had succeeded: reports in 1965 pointed out that 'working from seven small rooms' a squad of seven detectives and two assistants had cleared up over a thousand crimes in the period between February 1964 and March 1965. Most of the crimes solved were of housebreaking, receiving and robbery. The team in question was the one working in Surrey and South West London, Berkshire and Sussex. A journalist enquiring into the men's character and work noted that one detective 'admitted cheerily' that his work had brought him up against 'old school chums'. The main report in *The Times* was indeed a celebration, making the squad seem almost miraculously efficient, pointing out that the detectives had worked between '70 and 80 hours a week, spending as little time as possible in the office and as much time as possible working where the criminals are.' What summed up the triumph was the note that a case in Epsom had led to an arrest in Sheffield.

In the years between 1950 and 1965 then, the status and public image of the detective had been tarnished in several instances, but in such ever-present events as robberies and dramatic chases led by the Flying Squad, the detective was also perceived as a character belonging in a black and white B movie. There was also the notion of self-sacrifice bound up with the image of the police: *The Blue Lamp* featuring Dixon of Dock Green and a gathering of young officers and detectives who were pitted against the new, supposedly more ruthless criminal, and that good fight came to represent a whole tranche of traditional moral values. Arguably, in fact, the detective in the media and in film or fictional narrative was fixed somewhere between the gentlemanly Holmes and the more mundane dogged investigator wearing his mac and hat, walking down the 'mean streets'.

When Jack Slipper published his autobiography in 1981, the title was *Slipper of the Yard*. This phrase was set as a culturally evocative indicator of a certain type of man: organised, meticulous and yet with a dash of daring and courage. Criminals would fear anyone who was 'of the Yard'. Slipper himself pinpointed the special glamour of the Flying Squad, and they undoubtedly stole the limelight:

> The public image of the Squad as the 'heavy mob' is immensely valuable; to be known as a force that will do the job, however much resistance is put up … however much a villain argues or resists is very useful … Obviously this kind of image does cause some jealousy in other parts of the force; there is some rivalry with other units.

Slipper was well aware that there were detectives in that period who were easily placed alongside the characters in the movies, but was also aware of the men in the regions like Fraser who was shot in the Huddersfield surveillance, and Hall who led his effective but unsung team to investigate their local serial killer when that term and personality type was relatively unknown.

The history of the professional detective in the twenty years or so after the Second World War is particularly complex because the entire definition and identity of that figure was in flux. Holmes and Sexton Blake were there in the public image, together with the amateurs of Dorothy L. Sayers and Margery Allingham, but the range of gun crime and the new gangland outfits soon brought the dream narrative of the sleuth down to earth. He was moving into a broader amoral landscape and most of the gentlemanly virtues of the Edwardian age would have to go. Accountants, forensic scientists and administrators were to move into the scene, and arcane knowledge would have certain kudos along with the established virtues of courage, risk and intuition. Yet one development was endorsed as a fundamental element in the definition of a detective in those decades: he, or indeed she, was to be one of a team. The loners would still remain in fiction and there were the individuals and eccentrics who occasionally emerged, but in general it was a new world of teamwork and logistical fine-tuning from the establishment of the Regional Crime Squads and the backing they had in the science laboratories. After the shocks of the corruption cases on the one hand and the serial killer psychopaths on the other, a detective's daily work began to include a more voluminous stack of essential reading and a greater sensitivity to the notion that, as John Donne memorably wrote, 'No man is an island, entire of itself.'

The average regional officer, as opposed to the Yard man, had always just got on with the demands of routine, but in this period he would become acutely aware that mass communications, always changing the nature of crime, would inevitably change his own role and self-perceptions. His public image would also become very different: much of his work would become more visible and open to accountability when the television news cameras swung into action. The arrival of *Z Cars, Softly Softly* and the other early television dramas began the steady erosion of fact and fiction that would transmute all police work by the 1970s into something ostensibly in need of documentary representation. The mystique was about to take a bow.

But the present survey will end with a look at three detectives who broke the mould, and whose influence will always be there in detective work, as templates for certain persistent images and definitions.

12

CASE STUDIES IN CHARISMA

The years between 1950 and 1965 contain individual personalities as well as the chronicle of crime in a society of extreme deprivation and utilitarian recovery. In the history of the detective in that period, the personalities who attracted attention and found themselves often in the public eye help us to assemble another version of the emergence of the detective in England, and three men stand out as exemplars of those qualities in detective officers that remain a part of the elusive attraction of the public for such crime fighters. These are Herbert Hannam, Robert Fabian and Leonard Nipper Read.

On Coronation Day, 1 June 1953, the papers were busy with another story: a young girl named by many as 'The Force's Sweetheart' was brutally murdered by the Thames bank at Teddington on 31 May, and her body thrown into the river. This was sixteen-year-old Barbara Songhurst, and her best friend Christine Reid, also disappeared, her body being found eventually a week later, in the river at Richmond. The man called in to sort things out was DS Herbert Hannam of Scotland Yard. He is not one of the big names from the Yard: his name does not figure prominently in the reference books, yet this charismatic figure always did police work with style and panache, and some of his most high profile cases tell us a lot about the man and about the nature of extreme crime at the time. But charisma or not, there are questions to be asked about his career, even to the point of asking, did he play a part in having an innocent man hanged?

He was a career-man for sure. His son, Kenneth, was also in the force, and Hannam was happily married, living in Willesden and with a successful stint as a lecturer at Hendon Police College behind him, too. In the post-war years, he emerged as a currency specialist and was given some high-profile cases.

Hannam was a dapper man, always extremely well turned out; a photograph of him taken in 1957 shows a solidly built man, quite short, with a military bearing. He wears a trilby and a three-piece suit and his shoes shine with a regimental sparkle. It is an image of a man who means business.

Just before the Songhurst case, Hannam had been involved in a case at Eastbourne where there had been what looked like a double killing, and the popular end of the daily press mysteriously reported that Hannam was being helped by a certain Dr X and another enigmatic Dr Y. This is just the kind of sensation that followed Hannam wherever he went.

The Songhurst-Reid murders were particularly nasty, and poor Christine had been stabbed in the back and raped. Both girls had been attacked on the Thames towpath, and on a cycle path – a fact that was a main factor in tracking down the killer. After Barbara's body was found on the bank between Teddington Lock and Eel Pie Island, the search operation was massive, as police were desperate to find Christine.

Barbara was a blond and considered to be smart and brainy; her friend Christine was, in the words of her own mother, 'backward'. But the friends were outgoing types and loved to cycle around the area. On this fateful day they had left for a 'spin' just after seven p.m. Events were pieced together after a group of young men who had been camping near the spot said they had been with the girls until eleven that night. An electrician, Albert Sparks, told officers that he and his mates were with the girls and that they had all arranged to meet there after talking at Richmond on the previous Friday.

Another line of enquiry was with the American G.I's at Bushey Park camp, as Barbara had a penchant for writing and talking to soldiers. Hannam said that Barbara had pen-friends covering almost the entire world and was always prepared to correspond with lonely soldiers. She used to send her photo to most of them, and she had been seen dancing with a dark-skinned man, possibly an Indian, earlier that week-end. Hannam was sure that this man was an American at the camp.

The murderer had shown no mercy and the killing was remarkably savage. A coroner reported that the killer had wielded the knife with 'colossal strength'. Barbara had been stabbed three times in the back. But the attacker was also careless; blood was found on the grass nearby and Christine's shoes were also left there. Hannam was sure the other girl had been killed also and told *The Express* that he expected to find her body soon.

She was found, and it was a terrible sight. Uncannily, Barbara had been re-dressed after being attacked and stabbed; Christine was only five feet six, with dark brown curly hair. Police knew exactly what she had been wearing that Sunday: a yellow cardigan, dark blue serge slacks and white ankle socks with black shoes. She had been battered relent-lessly and knifed no less than ten times.

On 3 June, a lead was reported involving two men with scarred faces. But this went nowhere; the Thames was searched, and huge electro-magnets were used. Navy divers took part. Some intensive and thorough work went on under the guidance of Hannam. Not only were launches dragging the river; a large patch of grass was carefully scythed in the search for clues, police dogs were used, and two pairs of shoes were found.

Then came the link that proved to be the clincher, and led Hannam to Alfred Whiteway. The common factor between victims and killer was the cycling habit. Barbara's new maroon sports model (only recently purchased) was missing. Now, two women had been assaulted in Surrey – one of them raped – and Whiteway had been held on suspicion for that. He was a keen cyclist. He was a married man, and separated from his wife, he was back living with his parents and they provided the alibi.

All seemed well for the man, until a vigilant police officer, cleaning out a patrol car, found an axe hidden under a seat. He realised that the car was the one that recently had Whiteway in it. Forensic tests soon established that the axe had been used on the two girls. Whiteway con-fessed. He was hanged on 22 December that year by Albert Pierrepoint at Wandsworth. Hannam had got his man, after a long and very resourceful search and enquiry.

We have already met Hannam in his visit north to Halifax to work on the Emily Pye murder. While that did little to enhance his reputation, it did confirm the widely-held opinion that calling in the Yard meant that there would be a dash of colour and style in an investigation, something to keep the newspaper men happy.

The Halifax and Teddington cases are just two affairs in the Herbert Hannam casebook. He must have known that you win some and you lose some, but the Emily Pye case must have been a huge disappointment. He had arrived like a trouble-shooter to help out the divisional men, and had been frustrated. Even Holmes would have been beaten.

But the man the reporters loved showed only one side of Herbert Hannam. He was also heavily involved in two important cases in this decade which have gone into the chronicles of crime in a less clear-cut way, and in both these – the Bodkin Adams fiasco and the Rowlands execution – Hannam perhaps made some disastrous mistakes.

In the peaceful retirement haven of Eastbourne in 1950, Irish doctor John Bodkin Adams began to arouse suspicion. Through modern eyes, it would be easy to see him as an earlier version of Dr Shipman. Adams was beneficiary in many old people's wills and at an inquest into the death of Mrs Morrell, it was considered that she had killed herself by taking an overdose of a drug given by Adams. But there had been rumours; Adams received a Rolls Royce after her death and gained other gifts also. Enter Hannam, who liked to spend a lot of time interviewing suspects, generally being around the place, watching and learning.

Hannam's colleagues had come to call him The Count as he had a tight-lipped, haughty and aristocratic manner about him. When he met Adams, he perhaps met his match. The doctor played his cards close to his chest. But Hannam began a large-scale investigation at Eastbourne; rumours were that he had investigated 400 deaths. Eventually, Hannam noted that Adams, when cornered, had hinted at euthanasia, but the detective charged him with murder. His response has led to the enigma of this case: he said, 'Murder? Can you prove it was murder? She was dying in any event?'

This haste of Hannam's led to the eventual failure to convict. In a very high profile trial five years later, when a Mrs Hullett had died in similar circumstances, Hannam and his colleagues had clearly missed a crucial piece of evidence for the defence: some diaries kept by a nurse in the case. The defence lawyer Geoffrey Lawrence made mince-meat of the prosecution and Adams was free to go. The rest of his life was spent well away from the front line of the media: he had committed minor offences in relation to cremation procedure, and was struck off the General Medical Register until 1961.

But the case shows that Hannam tended to rush in with flair and media hype around him, and that was often to his cost. This was never more true than in the 1946 Manchester case of Walter Rowland, who was to die in the noose the next year, and may well have been hanged in error. The story of this doomed man is a salutary example for any study of murder investigation when sightings and testimonies are many but confusing, and once more, Herbert Hannam, The Count, was in the thick of things after the body of prostitute Olive Balchin had been found bludgeoned to death on a bomb site in Cumberland Street.

The affair seemed pretty clear-cut at first, when the police found that there was a man with a motive, and with a previous murder accusation in his track record. This was Walter Rowland, a man in his late thirties who had, he claimed contracted VD from Olive. But then the complications set in. One of these was the fact that Rowland had an alibi. He had been out at New Mills and then Stockport on the night of the killing, even to the point that the landlord had noted his time at his digs in Brunswick Street, where he had signed the register. Even more convincing, Rowland had claimed to see two police officers at The Wellington pub at a particular time, and this was confirmed, principally by Sergeant Jones.

There were also problems with a series of identifications and descriptions that night – everything from a man walking a dog to a sighting in a café – and the men in these accounts did not match Rowland. It was then that everything entered another level of interest when a certain David Ware in Walton gaol wrote a confession and a remarkably authentic account of the night spent with Olive up to the time of the murder. He even noted what films they had seen, and talked about a ten shilling note – a detail on the finding of her body that only the killer would know.

Enter The Count. He and Barratt of the Met interviewed Ware. This was to be the decisive moment for the fate of Rowland. He insisted that his first statements were true, but eventually gave in and said, 'Better turn it in.' An identification parade took place, and a Mr Macdonald, who had sold the hammer (the murder weapon) to a man that night, recognised no-one in the line-up. It seemed that Ware had read about the case in the newspaper and fantasised. Hannam checked out the cinema location and it was concluded that anyone in the street could have seen what films were on, and the posters matched Ware's account.

That was the end for Rowland. But odd things still linger about this investigation; Hannam had been to check on the lodging house regis-ter and it had been destroyed, he said. Why? The unhinged Ware later told Bristol police that he had killed a woman: he said he was always feeling an urge to hit women on the head. The central question to be asked about the detectives' actions is why Ware was not checked out more meticulously; even the note that his letter matched the Sunday, not the Saturday of the killing, would not be a problem if the man was mentally unstable, maybe having lucid moments in between other negative symptoms.

But it was all immaterial to Walter Rowland, who was hanged in Manchester by Albert Pierrepoint in February 1947. A twisted irony came into play, as he had been convicted of the murder of his daughter, back in 1934. His death sentence was reprieved. Ware hanged himself in his Broadmoor cell in 1954.

Herbert Hannam has figured as a minor player in several general works on crime history, and not always in a good light. But certainly there was in his personality something assertively egotistical fused with many of the dynamic and most desirable qualities that many of the top brass of the Yard would want to nurture in their detectives. Arguably, the cases he was involved with that turned out to be complex and con-troversial, were those in which certain human situations were evident in which his own brand of personal power and vanity had space to find exercise that was not always wholesome. After all, one of his qualities – again something generally a virtue in a detective – was the ability to have a degree of empathy or rapport with those who had crossed the line into illegality by force of personality. It could be argued that his real forte would have been in offender profiling, had that been in existence in the grey, deprived fifties when most violent crime was desperate, unglamorous and somehow done at the basic end of the spectrum.

Robert Fabian will always be the 'Fabian of the Yard' as in the thirty-nine films of that title. He was born in Ladywell in 1901 and joined the Metropolitan Police in 1921. From West End Central division he progressed to the CID and in the course of his career he picked up forty Commissioners Commendations, and outstanding in all his achievements is surely his disposal of an IRA bomb in 1939. This was at Piccadilly Circus on 24 June, when he saw a paper parcel on the kerb, and found ten sticks of gelignite inside; one stick had a fuse and detonator. He diffused the bomb and took it to Vine Street where he immersed it in water. There was 40oz of high explosive in the parcel. For that he was awarded the coveted King's Police Medal, along with a presentation of £15 from the Police Fund in a special ceremony – something he would have valued highly, though not for the cash. His cases are numerous and most gathered a patina of special drama and incident, including the arrest of the man who killed the gang leader, Charles the Acrobat in 1926 and, perhaps the most celebrated of all, the Antiquis case in 1947. He retired in 1947 and died in 1978.

Fabian was always busy mediating the nature of his profession, one week talking to the Royal Geographical Society on 'Behind the Scenes at Scotland Yard' and the next attracting controversy by expressing opinions on crime and law, as in his lecture in New York in 1954 in which he said that the 'coddling' of criminals in Britain and the USA was responsible for the increase in crime. He had several affectionate nicknames among his peers, including 'Fun and Games' because of his love of practical jokes, and 'Beau Brummel' due to his fame for attention to detail.

Such was his reputation that officers would say 'Fabian is on the job' and by that they meant that everyone expected an arrest. His attention to detail and his dogged persistence are illustrated in the Antiquis case. That murder appears entirely fitting as a case in which Fabian excelled, because the victim was a truly heroic and brave man who was in the mould of Fabian himself. Alec Antiquis was riding his motorcycle in Charlotte Street on the day when a gang decided to rob a jewellery shop in Tottenham Court Road. He was married with a family and was thirty-four; he had brought a child out from a house-fire and had also rescued a child from the path of a horse let loose in the streets. This brave man was in the way of the robbers, and was shot in the head at close range. He died shortly after reaching hospital.

The robbers had seemingly disappeared after a chase and there was very little to go on, with the added problem that witnesses in the crowded streets gave conflicting details of the criminals. Fabian took charge, went to the post-mortem, and started his investigation. There were no leads and nothing significant showed up in the ballistics study by Robert Churchill. But the first glimmer of hope that a lead might appear was when various witnesses agreed that they had seen men enter a flat at Brook House. Fabian's thoroughness was applied: the search of that property included a look at a small junk-room beyond the offices, and there detectives found an overcoat with cap, gloves and scarf. The tracking of the origins of the garments at first seemed to be impossible, but the mackintosh was made by Burton. The break came with the important fact that, because of black market trading, Burton's coats had numbers of ration-book holders sewn in the lining in order that they could be shown to be authentic products by Burton's company.

Fabian's team followed this lead and it led to a man called Kemp who was related to the Jenkins gang. As there was now a link to known robbers, there was hope of a 'result'. One Jenkins member was serving time, but the other was interviewed and from there the other gang members were found and arrested. It was still not an easy matter though, as Jenkins eluded an identity parade and had to be trailed. Three men – Jenkins, Geraghty and Rolt – were eventually charged. The first two hanged and Rolt was spared due to his youth. Witnesses with 'alibis' were not convincing, so Jenkins' last ploy was thwarted and he was doomed. Fabian won through his sheer terrier-like spirit and his attention to fine detail.

In contrast, Fabian had failures, notably an excursion into Warwickshire on a case that was bizarre and entirely suitable for his talents: it was a murder on St Valentine's Day, 1945, in the village of Lower Quinton. The victim was Charles Walton, a farm labourer seventy-four years of age. Charles was definitely a local 'character': he had lived there all his life and was known to have clairvoyant powers, including a 'magic touch' with animals. In fact, so talented was he in the wise ways of country traditional lore that some thought he had always dabbled in witchcraft.

On the fateful day of his killing, Charles was working on a place called Meon Hill, clipping some hedges; he had with him a bill hook and a pitchfork, and someone used that pitchfork to impale the poor man. He was found dead, and not only had he been stabbed with that tool, he also had a cross carved into the flesh of his chest. Fabian was sent for by the local police and the celebrity from the Yard came to work with two local CID men. What came out was a story, in print, about a murder carried out in exactly the same way, but the earlier tale led nowhere in the context of the modern killing. Fabian of the Yard had to admit defeat and went away with nothing to go on and no suspects, let alone any possible motives.

Fabian was always called upon for opinions, and in 1954 he used his column in a popular newspaper to join in the debate about the use of the 'cat' in punishment. He wrote:

Two convicts got the 'cat' in Wandsworth last week. You know what that means. They were strapped to an execution triangle and flogged. One man got eighteen strokes, the other six. Both convicts received this punishment for brutally attacking a prisoner officer and now both men are very unlikely to attack a prison officer again. Insurance assessors would give you long odds against it.

The feature shows Fabian in the familiar long overcoat and trilby, solid and dependable, representing Victorian values, advocating the kind of punishment that drove the British imperial armies into the disciplined actions that subdued the enemy.

The piece sums up what a large part of Fabian's appeal was. But that aspect is little known. What persists is the image of the man in the squad car, barking out orders and in control.

An anecdote told by Sam Jackett sheds light on the man's true charisma. After his bomb disposal exploit, he had a note saying he was expected at a pub in London. When he arrived, 'the biggest collection of thieves and rogues' was assembled. One man gave him a whisky and another a cigar. The crooks had made him a medal of their own, inscribed: 'To Robert Fabian for Heroism – from the boys.'

'I want you to get a little team together and have a go at the Krays.' That was what Leonard Read was told by his superior officer in 1964. He had been involved in the hunt for the Great Train robbers and when he started work on the Kray case he was not exactly sanguine in his hopes of a breakthrough. So many people linked with their protection rackets and other schemes were afraid to talk to the law, naturally. But he selected the men who were to make up his squad and set up camp at Tintagel House. Nothing could really be kept from the Krays if it is was happening in London, and they knew about Read. The link in the chain of potential informants broke when Leslie Payne spoke to the detectives and from that moment Read had a chance of success. It was all down to the assembling of the right men, on Read's part.

That was Nipper Read's fundamental skill: he knew people and assessed character very acutely. The Krays had stepped up to murder and Jack 'The Hat' McVitie had disappeared. There were suspicions of course, but the Krays escaped from the heat for a while, holidaying in Cambridge and Suffolk. It was then that Read was busy.

Read was a short man but he was strong and athletic; like the Krays, he was a useful boxer, and he had acquired that nickname of 'Nipper' in his early fighting days. He was only five foot seven but personality was his virtue and he had charisma. Promoted to Detective Superintendent, he set to work. He had found quick promotions in the Metropolitan Police and he was one of the youngest men to hold a senior position. But there were considerable obstacles in the Kray case. First, there was no evident collation of information about their criminal network. The men he chose were picked for specific talents: John de Rose was head of the Murder Squad and Frank Cater was chosen as Nipper's assistant. He set a target of three months to clear up the case.

The main elements in the operation were to help the essential unobtrusiveness by varying routes when at work; put a stress on the security of the team members and to explore the long trail of pain and devastation they had left in the lives of their victims in past years. Read sorted through the people in that history and ended with a list of thirty – his 'delightful index' as he called it. Read expressed the beginnings of this unique challenge in his memoirs: 'This is what always appalled me when I first started the enquiry. You'd talk to the CID officers and they'd say, "Oh this is down to the Krays" and you'd say, "Well what are you doing about it?" And the answer was they were doing nothing about it.'

As those involved were gradually interviewed, Read selected the best potential witnesses from his list, men like Sidney Vaughan. But his first arrest brought no-one to testify and in fact stirred some of the alleged Kray allies in the higher echelons, men like Lord Boothby, who had denied any relationship with the brothers in the press, other than 'business' relationships. But at that first arrest, he spoke in the House of Lords, expressing indignation at the apparent detention without trial that was suspected. The trial was a mess and ended in the frustration of a set re-trial. Read would have to work hard to get it right the next time.

The Krays thought they had won and went home to celebrate, but Read gave himself six months to be prepared for round two. The break came with Leslie Payne, who knew about the murder of McVitie and thought he was most likely to be next in line. Read had Payne protected by installing him in a hotel in Marylebone, and let him write a long statement of his knowledge of events around the Krays' 'business'. Read saw a lot of men personally, and many faded away, not interested in helping. But Payne was a key figure and here was huge success at last. Payne fitted into the Kray's empire as the financial brain. Read explained his role: 'He was the man who had made fortunes for the twins by setting up cells of Long Firm frauds. He was far more intelligent than most of those I saw, but I had to remember he was the most experienced, even brilliant, con-man.'

Payne admitted that it was the escalation of violence by the Krays that had turned him against them. Read met Payne several times and moved easily and sensitively towards having him on the side of law. The turning point was Read's question about whether Payne knew about 'The List'. That was the hit-list Ronnie had of those destined to be 'topped'. The way the twins worked in that context made sense to both men; after all McVitie had died because he kept money given to him by Kray in payment for a job – a job he did not do. Read took a 164-page statement from Payne, sat in a police section house in Marylebone.

Read then steadily gathered other witnesses, including Freddy Gore, and he was at pains to assure each person he approached that he would not be isolated, 'on a limb' as he testified. Such actions as wire-tapping then gave Read knowledge of some of the jobs effected by the twins up in Glasgow and elsewhere. He began to understand the extent of the web of criminality he was dealing with.

When ready to swoop, Read, with characteristic caution and preparation, held a pre-arrest briefing. He had to protect witnesses at the same time as he moved in, as there were so many unknown components in the Kray empire and no total trust in anyone who had spoken to him. He had cells prepared at West End Central Police Station; he checked with his surveillance teams, and then followed them back to their council flat in Shoreditch. The usual practice of an early approach, as suspects were off-guard, did the trick. Ronnie was in bed with a young boy and Reggie was with a girl. The arrest was low-key:

When I told Ronnie he was being arrested he said, 'Yes all right Mr Read, but I've got to have my pills, you know that'. He was referring to his supply of Stematol which kept him on an even mental keel. When Frank Cater told him he could not have them he pleaded with me and asked me to bring a letter from his psychiatrist which said he had to take two a day.

After that it was a case of tracking down the minor players. The triumph was Read's and this time he had witnesses in place, dependable and protected.

At the trial, Justice Melford Stevenson completed the process of justice – Ron went down for murdering Cornell and Reg for killing McVitie. The jury took six hours and fifty-four minutes to decide their guilt. Stevenson was the judge who sent the Krays to prison on thirty-year stretches. They were both defiant regarding Read, saying that he and other officers came to try to 'put the frighteners on them' and that they told him to 'fuck off'. Read's long and careful investigation had proved that the prevailing attitudes which accepted some powerful gangs as unassailable were defeatist and that they were in fact denying police work and taking the concept of professionalism down several pegs. He had the enterprise as well as the determination to take on the most powerful outfit in London and indeed beyond the city, as he gradually learned as the truth about the Kray empire.

According to some commentators, Read had also had to fight the 'mandarins on the fifth floor' at the Yard. Read was aware of some officers who had applied misguided loyalty to the wrong men. That footnote to his career only serves to increase the opinion that he was a 'reader of men' before he was anything else as a policeman. Clearly, Read was one of those detectives who had to work with total integrity in all contexts, as in the story of his being involved in a raid on a bookmakers in Albany Street when the phone rang with a fellow detective wanting to put a bet on. Tactfully and professionally, Read said, 'Sorry Sid, not today.'

Overall, Read, Fabian and Hannam may be said to represent different aspects of the special version of the Yard detective. They each had one notable quality that led to their success: Read had people skills in abundance; Hannam had flair and leadership integrity; and Fabian had glamour mixed with fearlessness. Each in his own way helped to create the sense that Scotland Yard did have a list of genuine and substantial achievements – things to override the too-numerous corruption scandals in the twenty years after the Second World War.

CONCLUSIONS

In his survey of the state of the police in 1964, Ben Whitaker included some comments on the notion of a national CID. He knew his facts about the new sense of co-operation across the country, noting that in 1962 'the Yard co-operated with other forces in over 1,700 cases – an increase of nearly 500 on the figure of the previous year.' He pinpoints the advantages by referring to France and notes what Sir Ronald Howe had said when suggesting that Britain follow the French *brigade mobile* method: 'Sir Ronald Howe suggests that a national CID here with their headquarters perhaps in Birmingham could have had 500 detectives searching for a hide-out within three hours of the big mail-train robbery.'

It was a thought that was in most policemen's minds: detectives in specialist squads were proving that such specialisms were the way forward. In this survey, the overview shows a series of quite amazing stages towards the professional expertise now accepted as integral to the role and function of a police detective. In the first phase, largely in the first two decades of the detective force, the learning curve was concerned with how to expand on the new practise of the uniformed officers and Bow Street Runners: the need to continue with the good application of informants and the cultivation of networks of criminals who were well aware of the new police and how to effect a compromise with them.

In that first phase, the established mode of selection of constables was vague and fundamental to say the least. The chief constable of Lincolnshire, a man who was so serious about his work that he wrote a code of conduct for officers and brought in a moral uprightness as part of the job description, appeared to watch every man in his county with exceptional vigilance, and his guidelines for recruitment were primarily to do with physical strength as one might find in a farm labourer, and the traditional English virtues of persistence and teamwork. Something of that has survived all the way to the current force.

A detective working in London around the year 1880 had something else to prove – that he was not corrupt and open to bribery. At the Trial of the Detectives of 1877, Baron Pollock, presiding, made a comment in his summing up that has resonated through the decades: 'It is indeed many years since in this country persons in your position were placed at a criminal bar charged with having betrayed a trust so important and solemn – a trust which was committed to you in the interests of your fellow citizens.' The word 'solemn' is the adjective charged with meaning there – fitting neatly into a quasi-religious or sacred context of meaning. That is, an oath was involved, and the following duty was one of taking on a status that had to be exemplary to others.

However, it has to be said that the 'first detective', Vidocq, had a profound influence on English conceptions of the profession, and he himself was a former criminal. James Morton has noted just how strong the impact of Vidocq on popular narrative in the ten years after the founding of the 'Peelers': he notes that after Vidocq's memoirs were published, the fascination with his life and career led to such creations as the play, *Vidocq The French Spy* at the Coburg Theatre, a typical melodrama of the age.

After the Ripper, Frederick Deeming the serial killer, and the Florence Maybrick affair, all in the 1880s and 1890s, the detective's image was to change for ever. Detectives may have failed to catch the Ripper but they had followed Deeming, a man who had had killed in Liverpool and in Hull, all the way to Australia and found his den, with bodies buried under the floor; he had been hanged in Melbourne and the chase had been across the globe. The link between the adventure story and the detective was well established. Not only the appearance of Holmes, but the popular Sexton Blake (who first appeared in *The Missing Millionaire: The Story of a Daring Detective* in 1893) shifted the detective into realms of the ripping yarns. Since Holmes and Blake, as David Stuart Davies has said, 'The world has been swamped by brilliant, idiosyncratic crime-solvers.'

Coming down to earth, a more realistic picture of a fairly typical career for a detective in London can be gleaned from that of Walter Dew, the key figure in the Crippen case. He had seen varied and demanding service in all kinds or urban police work, never particularly noticed. But he has established his own patterns of work and his own practices when it comes to handling criminals or definite suspects. The way he allegedly mishandled the Crippen investigation at the early stage is rather unfair; his decision to dine with Crippen and to try to study and understand the man's eccentric attitudes and obsession with minutiae is surely defensible. There was no substantial case against Crippen at the time – merely some irregularities and suspicions from Belle's friends. Spun another way, Dew was actually acting in advance of his time, attempting some amateur profiling.

The other major feature in this long history is the way in which adaptations were made as either major crimes occurred or when social change was so erratic and wayward that panic set in. Most historians would surely like to argue that it was a case of adapting to survive because, after all, demands made on the 'top brass' of detectives forces come from a multiplicity of sources. Not only does the Home Office demand attention and results, but the Third Estate of the papers and the 'Man on the Clapham omnibus' also wants a guarantee of safety around him. The panic of 1862, when the garrotting gangs were on the loose in London and in the regions, illustrates the pattern: minor attacks in the streets made theatre-goers making their way home extremely defensive, so that *Punch* was having fun inventing ridiculous means of self-defence against the gangs, and enjoying the satire of saying that the police were ineffectual against these thugs of the night.

Of course, the impact on detective work of the Ripper year cannot be underestimated. A read of the police reports at the time shows very powerfully exactly what was being asked of detective officers. They had to describe details immaculately; express themselves with tact and restraint, and be aware of not forgetting the obvious stages of an enquiry. In fact, it is clear that the Ripper investigations created a detective state of mind – something not seen before. Underneath the panic and sense of frustration, there was something crucially important going on in that horrendous regime of killing: a criminal psychopath was introducing the notion of a detective as a player in his fantasy microcosm. The image of the Peeler on the beat had little to do with that fantasy: it was (and still is) about a mind-game, and without the intellect of the lead officers – the Reads and Fabians – there would be no substance in the sick fantasies. Popular narrative and film today has magnified this interplay in the homicidal microcosm into a cliché, but the idea of the detective as a superior intellect persists.

In the novels of Val McDermid featuring Tony Hill, we have that theme taken into the latest psychological police work, something integrating both forensics and the knowledge of human motivation into the detection process. Interestingly, the profiler works both alone with inner resources and sheer instinct, and then with a team, as Dr Julian Boon does: he is 'The Real Cracker' and sees himself as a detective with a task of assembling a personality from fragments. Stephen Cook writing about Boon, explains: 'He has developed an approach where he regards nothing as irrelevant and tries to draw up a list of what he regards as the salient case details.' At the heart of this is the contemporary viewpoint of increasing use of instinct, patterning and even empathic thinking in detective work.

The idea of empathy has always been there, except that in the first decades of the detective it was based on a simple level of thought such as 'What would the killer do if … ?' Now, our age is one of classification, and we create these with the confidence only advanced human science can give.

One fundamental line of thought in this history is that detectives fall into categories. Some rely on a feeling for the motivations of their suspect, they have a 'nose' for detective work; others rely on systems, methods and established practices; others still have a military approach and see an investigation as a campaign. It is difficult to pick out what might have been the most successful formulae or ways of working. All that can be said is that long hours and patience are the recurring virtues selected to describe experienced officers when novice detectives write about their education in the force.

As with many things in the melting-pot of frenetic mid-Victorian London, Dickens had much right about the detective, but in concentrating on his descriptions of London men, his provincial excursions have been overlooked. In his collection of essays, *The Uncommercial Traveller*, Dickens goes to Liverpool. There he spends a night with the police and he has some fun at the expense of the sleuths: he goes with two officers, calling them Sharpeye and Mr Superintendent, and he delights in watching their methods; they were hunting for a man called Mercantile Jack:

> So Sharpeye before and Mr Superintendent and I went next ... Sharpeye, I soon had occasion to remark, had a skilful and quite professional way of open-ing doors ... Sharpeye opened several doors of traps that were set for Jack but Jack did not happen to be in any of them.

Dickens had seen and understood the nature of crime detection in Victorian cities: sheer dogged routine and the inspection of known locales and felons. He saw the fruitless, vapid work, tiring and dispiriting. He ends the piece by saying that he had seen 'vermin' and that 'vermin were running all over my sleep.'

The detective officer at that time, around 1855, was more often the scruffy, overtired Liverpool 'Sharpeye' than the glamorous and dangerous characters in the London sketches he wrote, giving his readers a more fictional account of the detectives in their 'club' milieu, discussing villains and methods.

Conclusions to be drawn from this history are all related to the persistence of misconceptions. As the media developed and kept pace with the needs of the society they served, the representations of detectives were always caught between the real and the ideal. Fabian commenting on actual aspects of the penal system for a national daily was a thousand miles beyond the comprehension of men like Abberline in the Victorian period, who would have felt a shiver of apprehension at the thought of a newspaper man following them with a notebook flapping and a string of questions being voiced.

A turning point in the roles of detectives was the Great War and the years immediately before its beginning. When Vernon Kell initiated his interceptions of mail for cases of suspected spies, the advice and support that he received from the CID was a truly significant departure. In 1911, Winston Churchill, then the Home Secretary, issued general warrants permitting that interception. The following work involved support from a former head of the CID, Edward Drew, and under his cover the department could work, with Drew acting the role of a private detective. It is not hard to argue that this invited all kinds of new and uncomfortable roles for detectives. Henceforth, because they had to work in surveillance of 'ordinary people' who may or may not have been spies, they found themselves immersed in the kind of close detection that involves everything from searching dustbins to snooping into eating and shopping habits. On many occasions, they read personal and intimate letters between lovers or between man and wife.

It was inevitable that a code of practice with an eye to the moral respon-sibilities of the job should emerge. The 1938 report has nothing particular to say on the matter, but it is something that has never gone away and every case of bribery impinges on that delicate area.

The matter of women detectives is an aspect of the overall history that has never been prominent in the years covered here. In 1938 the only reference to the subject in the vast report was this:

> We recognise that women can be employed with advantage in some varieties of detective enquiries, but we have not found sufficient evidence of the need for the employment of police women as detective officers to justify a departure from the principle followed hitherto, that the employment of women on police work should be a matter for the discretion of the Individual Chief Officers …

In other words, no decision as yet and this is not a priority, thank you. That was the attitude. In 1962 a working party looked into the organisation of the CID in terms of the waste of manpower and another working party looked at women's roles in the police. The Yard announced in June of that year that women were to be encouraged to become detectives, and that some would be appointed as aides to detective work. They would work for a probationary period and then take a ten-week course. To train as a detective a female applicant had to have served fifteen months in uniform and have passed a probationers' course. Those women detectives already in place as sergeants were also given the go-ahead to transfer to uniform branches. At least there was some evidence there, at the end of the period covered here, that a revolution was on the way.

That finally started to happen in 1972, as in that year Scotland Yard decided to put an end to the existence of the separate women's police force. Women officers were from that point to be integrated into the Metropolitan Police structure. The first stage was to transfer women into community relations duties and into management services. Sir Robert Mark, then Commissioner, told the press that 'The role of women in the police has been under discussion for some time. Various groups, including the Police Federation, have been consulted.' In a statement that through modern eyes resonates with prejudice, it was said that women would 'be able to reach whatever rank was within their capability.' At the time there were around 600 women in the police, and they had been in the CID in various capacities since 1907, but it took until 1923 for women to be given the same status and powers as policemen. A final reform was the promotion of the country's senior policewoman, Commander Shirley Brooke, to the inspectorate.

Women in detective work were often employed in one of the most dangerous roles of all: decoys in operations. Women officers had won the George Medal in some decoy work, but that never really made the headlines as much as it deserved to do.

The major conclusion after this survey has to be that through modern eyes, with so much sophisticated science and methodology now in detective work, the growth of the detective in England has been primarily a record of magnificent achievement, by both men and women, in every imaginable context of criminal law, and the demands on those officers goes on accelerating every day.

BIBLIOGRAPHY

Contemporary Books and Articles

Unless stated, place of publication for all titles is London.

Books:

Aston, Sir George, *Secret Service* (Faber and Faber, 1930)

Caminada, Jerome, *Caminada the Crimebuster* (True Crime Library, 1996)

Cherrill, Fred, *Cherrill of the Yard: The Autobiography of Fred Cherrill* (Harrap, 1955)

Criminal Appeal Records, Sweet and Maxwell (annual) various consulted

Denning, Lord, *Landmarks in the Law* (Butterwoths, 1984)

Dernley, Syd, with Newman, David, *The Hangman's Tale: Memoirs Of a Public Executioner* (Robert Hale, 1989)

Dickens, Charles, *Hunted Down: The Detective Stories of Charles Dickens* (Peter Owen, 1996)

Dickens, Charles, *Reprinted Pieces* (Chapman and Hall, 1907)

Dickens, Charles, *The Uncommercial Traveller* (Chapman and Hall, 1880)

Ensor, David, *I Was a Public Prosecutor* (Robert Hale, 1958)

Fraser, Frankie, with Morton, James, *Mad Frank's Britain* (Virgin, 2003)

Hastings, Macdonald, *The Other Mr. Churchill: A Lifetime of Shooting and Murder* (Four Square Books, 1963)

Hastings, Sir Patrick, *Autobiography* (Heinemann, 1948)

Hawkins, Henry, *The Reminiscences of Sir Henry Hawkins* (Nelson, 1910)

Home Office report of the departmental Committee on Detective Work and Procedure (HMSO, 1938)

Humphreys, Sir Travers, *Criminal Days: Recollections and Reflections* (Hodder and Stoughton, 1946)

Humphreys, Sir Travers, *A Book of Trials: Personal Recollections of an Eminent Judge of the High Court* (Pan, 1953)

Mortimer, John, *Where There's a Will* (Penguin, 2004)

Morton, James, *The First Detective: The Life and Revolutionary Times of Vidocq, Criminal and Master Spy* (Ebury Press, 2004)

Nield, Basil, *Farewell to the Assizes* (Garnstone Press, 1972)

Punch Library in Wig and Gown (Educational Book Co., 1920)

Read, Leonard, with Morton, James, *Nipper Read: The Man Who Nicked the Krays* (Time Warner, 1991)

Report of the Royal Commission on Police Powers and Procedure (HMSO, 1929)

Richardson, Charlie, *My Manor: An Autobiography* (Pan, 1991)

Slipper, Jack, *Slipper of the Yard* (Sidgwick and Jackson, 1982)

Smith, Sir Sydney, *Mostly Murder* (Odhams Press, 1959)

Trigg, Chief Superintendent W., *Lincolnshire Constabulary Instruction Book* (Henry Slack: Lincoln, 1920)

Young, Hugh, *My Forty Years at the Yard* (W.H. Allen, 1955)

Articles:

Anderson, Patrick W., 'The Death of a Detective' in *Journal of the Police History Society* No.19, 2004, pp.8–10

Bebbington, Sarah, 'Watching the Detectives' in *Police Review* 16 June 2006, pp.20–21

Day, Joanna, 'Herbert Hannam's Narrow Squeak' in *Master Detective* September 1994, p.51

Lambourne, G., 'A Brief History of Fingerprint Identification' in *Journal of the Police History Society* No.1, 1986

Pentland, A., Detective Inspector, 'Detective's Portable Forensic and Finger-Print Outfit,' in *Police Journal* Spring 1935

Welsh, David, 'Nineteenth Century Policemen as Workers: The Moulding of a Police Force in Hull *c.*1836–1866' in the *Journal of Regional and Local Studies* Vol.20 No.2, Winter 2000, pp.3–27

Wright, Norman, and Ashford, David, 'Enter Sexton Blake' in *Book Collector* January 2007, pp.72–81

Journals and Periodicals:

Annual Register March 1857, on James Seward.

The Daily Mail

Halifax Courier

Household Narrative

Illustrated London News

Real Life Crimes

Social History

The Police Review

The Times Digital Archive 1785–1985

True crime Magazine

Secondary Sources:

Books:

Baker, J.H., *An Introduction to English Legal History* (Butterworth, 2002)

Beavan, Colin, *Fingerprints: Murder and the Race to Uncover the Science of Identity* (Fourth Estate, 2003)

Begg, Paul, and Skinner, Keith, *The Scotland Yard Files: 150 Years of the C I D* (Headline, 1992)

Bingham, John, *The Hunting Down of Peter Manuel, Glasgow Multiple Murderer* (Macmillan, 1973)

Bloom, Clive, *Violent London: 2,000 years of Riots, Rebels and Revolts* (Pan Books, 2004)

Boghardt, Thomas, *Spies of the Kaiser: German Covert Operations in Great Britain during the First World War Era* (Palgrave, 2004)

Browne, Douglas G., *The Rise of Scotland Yard* (Harrap, 1956)

Campbell, Christie, *Fenian Fire: The British Government Plot to Assassinate Queen Victoria* (HarperCollins, 2003)

Cobb, Belton, *Critical Years at the Yard* (Faber and Faber, 1946)

Cobb, Belton, *The First Detectives* (Faber and Faber, 1957)

Cook, Stephen, *The Real Cracker: Investigating the Criminal Mind* (Channel Four Books, 2001)

Crimebusters, Time Warner [no author given] (1989)

Cyriax, Oliver, *The Penguin Encyclopaedia of Crime* (Penguin, 1996)

Davey, B.J., *Lawless and Immoral: Policing a Country Town 1838–1857* (Leicester University Press, 1983)

Davies, David Stuart, (Ed.) *Shadows of Sherlock Holmes* (Wordsworth Classics, 1998)

D'Cruze, Shani, Walklate, Sandra, and Pegg, Samantha, *Murder* (Willan Publishing: Cullompton, 2006)

Deans, R. Storry, *Notable Trials: Romances of the Law Courts* (Cassell, 1906)

Dell, Simon, *The Victorian Policeman* (Shire: Princes Risborough, 2004)

Diamond, Michael, *Victorian Sensation* (Anthem Press, 2004)

Dilnot, George, (Ed.) *The Trial of the Detectives* (Geoffrey Bles, 1928)

Dineage, Fred, *Reg and Ron Kray: Our Story* (Pan, 1989)

Eddlestone, John J., *The Encyclopaedia of Executions* (John Blake, 2002)

Emsley, Clive, *Crime and Society in England 1750–1900* (Longmans, 1987)

Emsley, Clive, *The English Police: A Political and Social History* (Longmans, 1996)

Evans, Stewart P. and Keith Skinner, *Jack the Ripper and the Whitechapel Murders* document pack (The National Archives, 2004)

Evans, Stewart P., and Skinner, Keith, *The Ultimate Jack the Ripper Sourcebook* (Robinson, 2000)

Fido, Martin, and Skinner, Keith, *The Official Encyclopaedia of Scotland Yard* (Virgin, 1999)

Firmin, Stanley, *Men in the Shadows: The Story of Scotland Yard's Secret Agents* (Hutchinson, 1953)

Goodman, Jonathan, *The Medical Murders* (Warner Books, 1991)

Hale, Leslie, *Hanged in Error* (Penguin Special, 1961)

Harrison, J.F.C., *Early Victorian Britain, 1832–51* (Fontana, 1988)

Hattersley, Roy, *The Edwardians* (Abacus, 2004)

Hobbs, Dick, *Doing the Business: Entrepreneurship, The Working Class and Detectives in the East End of London* (OUP: Oxford, 1989)

Hodge, James H., *Famous Trials 3* (Penguin, 1950)

Hoskins, Percy, *No Hiding Place! The Full Authentic Story of Scotland Yard in Action* (Daly Express publications, 1955)

Jackett, Sam, *Heroes of Scotland Yard* (Robert Hale, 1965)

Jackson, Stanley, *The Old Bailey* (W.H. Allen, 1978)

Jones, Richard Glyn, *True Crime and History* (Constable and Robinson, 1989)

Joyce, James Avory, *Justice at Work: The Human Side of the Law* (Pan Books, 1955)

Koestler, Arthur, and Rolph, C.H., *Hanged by the Neck* (Penguin Special, 1961)

Lane, Brian, *The Encyclopaedia of Forensic Science* (Headline, 1992)

Leech, T.J., *A Date with the Hangman* (True Crime Library, 1992)

Lock, Joan, *Dreadful Deeds and Awful Murders: Scotland Yard's first Detectives 1829–1878* (Barn Owl Books: Taunton, 1990)

Low, Donald A., *The Regency Underworld* (Sutton: Stroud, 2005)

McCarthy, Denis, *Dublin Castle: At the Heart of Irish History* (Government of Ireland: Dublin, 2004)

Morton, James, *Supergrasses, Informers and bent Coppers Omnibus* (Timewarner, 2002)

Moss, Alan and Skinner, Keith, *The Scotland Yard Files: Milestones in Crime Detection* (The National Archives, 2006)

Nown, Graham, *Watching the Detectives: The Life and Times of the Private Eye* (Grafton Books, 1994)

Odell, Robin, *The International Murderers' Who's Who* (Headline, 1996)

Ousby, Ian, *The crime and Mystery Book: A Reader's Companion* (Thames and Hudson, 1979)

Parris, J.M., and Crossland, John R., *The Fifty Most Amazing Crimes of the Last Hundred Years* (Odhams Press, 1936)

Prendergast, William, *Calling All Z Cars* (John Long, 1966)

Prothero, Margaret, *The History of the Criminal Investigation Department At Scotland Yard from the Earliest Times to Today* (Herbert Jenkins, 1931)

Rawlings, Philip, *Crime and Power: A History of Criminal Justice 1688–1998* (Longmans, 1999)

Readers' Digest: *Great Cases of Scotland Yard Vol 1* (Reader's Digest, 1978)

Rhodes, Linda *et alia*, *The Dagenham Murder: The Brutal Killing of PC George Clarke, 1846* (London Borough of Barking and Dagenham, 2005)

Richardson, Anthony, *Nick of the River: The Story of Detective Inspector Nixon, Late of the Thames Division, Metropolitan Police* (Harrap, 1955)

Smith, David James, *Supper with the Crippens: A New investigation into The Most Notorious Domestic Murder in History* (Orion, 2005)

Sugden, Philip, *The Complete History of Jack the Ripper* (Robinson, 1995)

Thomas, Donald, *The Victorian Underworld* (John Murray, 1998)

Thomas, Donald, *Villains' Paradise: Britain's Underworld from the Spivs to The Krays* (John Murray, 2005)

Tibballs, Geoff, *The Murder Guide to Great Britain* (Boxtree, 1994)

Tobias, J.J., *Crime and Industrial Society in the Nineteenth Century* (Penguin, 1967)

Ward, Jenny, *Crimebusting: Breakthroughs in Forensic Science* (Blandford, 1998)

West, Nigel, *MI5* (Grafton Books, 1997)

Whitaker, Ben, *The Police* (Penguin Special, 1964)

Wise, Sarah, *The Italian Boy: Murder and Grave-Robbery in 1930s London* (Pimlico, 2005)

Woodley, Mick, *Osborn's Concise Law Dictionary* (Thomson, 2005)

Web Sites:

www.crimelibrary.com/gangsters
www.cityoflondon.police.uk/aboutus/force-history
www.met.police.uk/so/special-branch
www.met.police.uk/history/timeline
www.murderfiles.com

NOTES TO PICTURES

Note: all acknowledgements for permission to reprint are given here as the sources. As explained in the introduction, the Percy Hoskins copyright holders have not been traceable, even with the help of Getty Images specialists.

1   Sir Richard Mayne, the first Joint Commissioner, working with Charles Rowan. He was sole Commissioner from 1855 until his death in 1868. (Laura Carter)

2   Superintendent Adolphus Williamson. He was the first senior officer in the CID. 'Dolly', as he was affectionately known, was a protégé of the great Jonathan Whicher, whom Dickens knew. (Laura Carter)

3   Chief Inspector Nathaniel Druscovich. One of the officers at the centre of the 'Trial of the Detectives'. He was of Polish extract and excelled in languages and in his sartorial elegance. (Laura Carter)

4   Townsend, one of the most famous of the Bow Street Runners. His most distinguished service was as a 'minder' of the King George III. (Author's collection)

5   Frontispiece of Colquhoun's book on police reform. His only satisfaction in terms of measures actually implemented was the formation of the river police.

6   'Inspector Field confronted with an unexpected clue.' An anonymous illustration from a serialised feature in a popular periodical.

7   Inspector Frederick Abberline. He served twenty-five years in the Metropolitan Police. He was transferred to Scotland Yard in 1887. (Alan Moss Collection)

8   Scalby Manor, Scarborough – home of the bloodhounds used in the Ripper hunt

9   Poster: 'Attempt to Assassinate the Queen.' Teenager Edward Oxford was the culprit. He fired his pistol at the Queen's head, but Albert saved her. (Author's collection)

10 James J. Thomson. He was a skilled linguist, active against the Fenian, John Groves. (Laura carter)

11 The 'Rookery' St Giles, 1850 (old print.) The rookeries were notoriously no-go areas for the police. Often they were the hiding places for deserted soldiers and mendicants

12 The old House of Detention, Clerkenwell. Later the scene of the Fenian bombing. A daunting place, housing all categories of prisoners. (From an old print)

13 Dublin Castle: headquarters of the detective force active against Fenians.

14 Sherborne Hotel, Dublin, where detectives were recruited by Jenkinson.

15 Thomas Holmes, the author of *Pictures and Problems from London Police Courts*. (1900). He was a valuable source of information for detectives, having made it his life's work to know and understand the 'underclass'. (Author's collection)

16 Parody detective story from the periodical *The Idler* (1900). Holmes had spawned his imitators by that time, and parodies were often indicative of the popular image of the detective. (Author's collection)

17 Officers at the Moat Farm Murder. This shows the uniformed and detectives at the investigation at Clavering in Essex. Sergeant Scott (seated, left) is the detective in charge. (Essex Police Musuem)

18 Gustav Steinhauer in police uniform before the First World War. He was instructed by the German Admiralty to conduct spy operations abroad and he came up against Vernon Kell and his MI5. Scotland Yard team. (Author's collection)

19 Dr Crippen. (Laura Carter)

20 Hilldrop Crescent, Crippin's house where Belle's body was found.

21 Inspector Walter Dew, the man who arrested Crippen. (Laura Carter)

22 London and North East detectives as Kings Cross 1940s. (John Bond, Northamptonshire police)

23 A hypothetical investigation at Hendon Detective Training. As part of 'X's' training, he is shown the relics of past crimes. Many of these exhibits were originally in Scotland Yard's Black Museum.

24 Detectives taking plaster moulds. This is from a training course on taking footprints and fingerprints. (Percy Hoskins)

25 First move by pupil 'X' is to take full details of the crime, noting in particular the position of the dead man and the state of the clothing.(Percy Hoskins)

26 Scene from the training course for detectives: The 'body' of a victim of a hit-and-run driver is inspected. (Percy Hoskins)

INDEX